Contents

Editorial

In this issue of *Gender and Development*, the topic of transition is viewed from a gender perspective; this means widening the term far beyond its current use in denoting the shift to market economics by formerly centrally-planned economies. At a time of escalating political and economic crisis, and growing conflict, it is important for development workers and activists within the women's movement to look as comprehensively as possible at the nature of change faced by women, at the material and emotional results of such change, and at possible ways forward. *Gender and Development* therefore explores transition in a holistic and inclusive sense, as a 'passing or change from one place, state or condition to another' (Oxford Dictionary, 1990).

The process of transition – whether the upheaval is perceived to be a result of international economic policy, of a change of political system, or of a shift in cultural or religious beliefs – throws down a challenge to the women and men who pass through it. Transition via the imposition of market economics – invariably allied to the introduction or reinstatement of so-called representative democracy – has brought significant change to many societies in the last decade. While some women, in possession of more resources, may have gained from economic and political transitions over the past decade since the Forward Looking Strategies were agreed in Nairobi in 1985, on the whole women have lost out. This is because women throughout the world are experiencing economic and political change, and the crisis which may result, differently from the men in their communities, due to their lack of power and status, and to beliefs governing 'appropriate' female behaviour. As Ines Smyth asserts in her article in this issue, 'change is intrinsic in human life. It opens the way to progress, but also contains the germ of uncertainty, hence insecurity.' Transition threatens the livelihoods and well-being of those social groups, including women, who have fewest resources and are excluded from decision making.

'The "free market" has little time for social or economic justice or notions of sustainable development (WIDE 1995).' Treating global transition as a single theme can be the first step to working together to address crisis: common areas in women's experience of poverty can form a basis for organised resistance. Integrating a gender perspective into development planning and policy highlights the social cost to poor women of imposing the draconian formulas associated with economic restructuring.

Challenging increasing poverty

International financial institutions have asserted that the neo-liberal economic policies of structural adjustment packages are designed to increase women's opportunity to earn income through participation in a reformed market. However, a close scrutiny reveals that it is not the poorest women who are able to participate in such markets. In this issue, two articles illustrate this point, in very different ways. First, in their article focusing on indigenous organisations of women traders in Techiman Market, Ghana, Carolyne Dennis and Ernestina Peprah highlight the constraints preventing the poorest women from participating in the expanded market which has resulted from Ghana's Economic Recovery Programme (ERP), introduced in 1984.

Second, the ways in which economic and political transition are affecting women are related to stereotypical male and female roles, which are re-established once poverty and unemployment threaten, as Maxine Molyneux's essay describes. In countries of the former Eastern Bloc, women's jobs have been the first to go and they have been forced back to their 'traditional' role of stay-at-home wife and mother. The state ceases to protect women's rights to employment outside the home, and the emergence of a new 'civil society' movement will have to pledge a stronger form of support for women who never shed their domestic responsibilities under Communism.

Migration to find employment is an increasing response to poverty and unemployment. In Susan Cueva's experience of the Philippines, becoming a migrant worker may be viewed by women as a path to autonomy; but gender ideology at home and in the host country all too often ensures that migrant workers experience another facet of poverty, far from any supportive networks. Susan Cueva's chosen topic also illustrates that in trying to meet the needs of themselves and their families, women may find they also face crisis in their relations with men, as increased domestic violence forces women to reassess whether they dare to continue to earn outside the home.

Conflict, survival and risk

As Judy El-Bushra and Cécile Mukarubuga state in their article drawing on the experience of ACORD, the UK-based NGO, of working with women in Rwanda, 'war represents transition in its most violent and bewildering form.' They call for new thinking on the issues, and speak of the need to 'construct new models from unfolding realities and to search for new insights rather than adhere to stereotypes.'

If we wish to understand women's chances of weathering crisis, and moving on to use change to improve their status and well-being, we must appreciate not only the complexity of women's lives, but how their vision of what is achievable changes according to their resources and the security of the external environment. Sebsted and Grown's 'livelihood strategies' model (Sebsted and Grown 1989) can be transferred from its original use as an analysis of income-generating in peace-time to become a useful tool in understanding the possibilities and constraints inherent in people's behaviour during post-conflict reconstruction. They make the critical, but often overlooked, point that women's attitude to taking risks in order to improve their livelihood is influenced by the resources – including education, material possessions and kinship – on which they can draw. Due to women's subordinate position in society, these tend to be fewer than men's: 'if a person has few special skills, no working capital and no influential friends, [her] bargaining power is usually very low...' (Gerry and Bromley 1979, 12). In distinguishing three main stages in making a livelihood – survival, stability and growth – Sebsted and Grown assert that, in times of crisis, women may find it more rational to consolidate the few resources they have, rather than to risk losing them through, for example, deciding to return home after being a refugee. Currently, research is needed into issues of risk, and the ways in which trust within a shattered community can be built up once more.

Challenging stereotypes may also be necessary in relation to male and female identities. Although it may be possible to challenge oppressive aspects of gender relations in the atmosphere of questioning that conflict and its aftermath create, it is also often the case that women and men's roles are even more polarised by conflict. El-Bushra and Mukarubuga point out that women's 'buttress' role in communities – shielding families and communities from shocks and disruption – is 'constrained by the stresses that they themselves come under during conflict, creating tensions not only for the women themselves but for their entire society'.

Redefining democracy

A cry during the recent Mozambiquan elections was that 'there can be no democracy without money!' In order to achieve justice and freedom from poverty for those who are marginalised from political decision-making and the policy-formulation of international financial institutions, there is a need to challenge not only the globalisation of neo-liberal economics, but also Western-style multi-party democracy.

As Ines Smyth asserts, women and other groups who are marginalised from decision-making are the most vulnerable in times of transition because they have the least say in the decisions which lead to such change. A critical resource for 'starting over' after crisis such as conflict is confidence in the new political structure. It is hard for people to have confidence in any political system which is not of their making. Ruth Jacobson examines women's political participation in Mozambique's 1994 elections and the ways in which voter education attempted to involve women as a constituency in the elections.

A different problem is posed for women by political transition in Algeria, where conservative political forces represent a threat to women's autonomy. In her article, Imane Hayef explores women's attitudes to politics and multi-partyism in the lead-up to the forthcoming election.

'Internal' transition

Women's status and welfare is not only challenged by transition imposed by external forces, but through the 'internal' transition of ageing. For women, this has far greater implications than for men; since women in most societies continue to be defined by their family role, whereas men achieve their status through activity in the public sphere. Whereas in the past older women may have been venerated for wisdom and maturity, the global spread of values based on modernisation and materialism tends to cause a change in the attitude of society towards its older members. In her article, Kasturi Sen explores the way in which conventional economic statistics, together with social prejudice, combine to marginalise older women. Just as women's unpaid work is ignored in statistics, so, too, older women are seen as a drain on society, because their massive contribution to production and reproduction is unrecognised. Sen argues that the women's movement, by failing to question prevailing values, has contributed to the marginalisation of older women – which amounts to a double disempowerment.

Working in change

Understanding change, and the ways in which development and relief work diverts or smooths the path which societies are taking, is vital if interventions are to benefit the societies in which agencies and NGOs work. It is profoundly difficult to entertain the idea that change cannot be predicted; 'there is no such thing as *the* future: the future is *always* unknown' (Morgan 1986, 272). Accepting this necessitates a completely new form of forward planning, which stresses learning from our experience, building capacity to cope with the unexpected – within ourselves and within the structures of our organisations – and making sure that we remember that development is a process rather than a set of 'before and after' snapshots.

For development agencies concerned with the empowerment of women, and for women's organisations working in South and North, coping with the challenges posed by transition means that 'instead of attempting to deal solely with events produced by different types of change, we must try to shape and guide the forces which produce such events, in order to change the nature of change itself' (Roche 1994, 170).

Intervening to change the course of development requires an analysis of the complex ways in which economic, political, and cultural factors interact to create transition and crisis; but we must remember that tracing the cause of transition may prove impossible, because of the complexity of the interactions, and because our own biases and beliefs affect our understanding of the processes of change.

Reflecting this, participants at a workshop held by Oxfam UK/I to explore ways of working in Cambodia during transition from conflict to peace stressed the importance of a 'balance between the need for long-range planning and the ability to respond flexibly to rapid and unpredictable change in our ways of working' (internal workshop report, Oxfam 1995).

For communities themselves, national governments, and international bodies, looking at different facets of change, and attempting to understand the broad trends which underlie them, is essential in order to halt the process of impoverishment and disempowerment which accelerates in societies in transition. Non-governmental organisations have multiple roles to play, to forestall and alleviate crisis. These include continuing long-term research on various forms of change, and using this in lobbying on the effects of large-scale transition on women. Women must play a more active role in decision-making, in political, financial, and development institutions. As we pass the landmark of the UN Fourth Conference on Women in Beijing, the governments of the world are under increasing pressure from the women's movement to take note of the complex links between the different forms of change and crisis faced by the world's women.

Caroline Sweetman

References

Gerry and Bromley (1979) (eds) *Casual Work and Poverty in Third World Cities*, Wiley.

Morgan G (1986) *Images of Organisation*, Sage: London.

Roche C (1994) 'Operationality in turbulence: the need for change', in *Development in Practice* 4: 3, Oxfam UK/I:Oxford.

Sebsted J and Grown C (1989) 'Towards a wider perspective on women's employment' in *World Development* 17: 7.

WIDE (1995) *Living and Working: An Illustration of the Feminisation of Poverty in Europe*, WIDE: Belgium.

Gender, change and insecurity

theoretical issues and practical concerns

Ines Smyth

In recent times, structural changes worldwide have led to spiralling insecurity for the most vulnerable people in society, the poor, women, and children. Change is intrinsic in human life. It opens the way to progress, but also contains the germ of uncertainty, hence insecurity.[1]

According to Drèze and Sen, the lives of many people are plagued by insecurity:

The lives of billions of people are not merely nasty, brutish and short, they are also full of uncertain horrors. An epidemic can wipe out a community, a famine can decimate a nation, unemployment can plunge masses into extreme deprivation, and insecurity in general plagues a large part of mankind with savage persistence.
Drèze and Sen, 1991:3

Insecurity has a personal dimension, in that it is experienced differently and to varying degrees by each individual. But it has also a structural dimension, since the overall conditions under which people live can eliminate or at least reduce such insecurity, or exacerbate it. Insecurity in some case is endemic, and where precariousness is superimposed onto deprivation (Burgess and Stern 1991), this combination gives rise to conditions which not only have an impact on daily life, but also profoundly affect the long-term prospects of individuals and communities, and future generations.

This paper is concerned with women for two reasons. One is to counteract the conventional neglect of women's needs and contributions with respect to security (Tickner 1992:53). The second is that a focus on women allows for a broader understanding of insecurity than would otherwise be possible. The 'realist' tradition of international relations equates insecurity with military threats, and in so doing centres its attention on the role of nation states and great powers (Grant 1991).

According to the critics of such a position, this understanding of insecurity is both too narrow and out of tune with recent events on the international arena. For them, this conventional understanding can be both broadened and brought up to date by the infusion of a gender perspective: a perspective that takes into consideration the views and experiences of women.[2] According to Tickner, this broader perspective shows that:

Many forms of insecurity in the contemporary world affect the lives of individuals, including ethnic conflict, poverty, family violence and environmental degradation.
Tickner 1992:127.

Before proceeding to analyse the specific case of women in relation to insecurity, it is important to repeat that economic, political and social structural changes are related to each other in complex ways. For example, conflict will certainly cause a deterioration in economic conditions, and bring damage to and neglect of the physical and natural environment, and thus will endanger the long-term prospect for regaining material security. Furthermore, the impact of such changes is extremely varied, depending on the type and extent of the transformations societies are undergoing, and on their pace.

Women and global insecurity

A focus on women's increased insecurity in the context of structural changes is not meant to imply either that men are immune from the negative effects that such transformations may bring about, nor that women are innately more vulnerable. It is the aim of this section to investigate the diverse mechanisms by which structural changes affect men and women differently. Another aim is to show the ways in which women have actively responded to these changes. To echo a statement made with reference to women and development more generally, discus-sions of insecurity need to take account of the choice and circumstance, and to treat [Third World] women not as passive, exotic victims, of either external forces or local conditions, but rather as active participants in change (De Groot 1991:123).

Economic insecurity

While insecurity may be part of the human condition, it has increased in recent years, for a number of inter-related reasons. One reason is the global economic crisis, which in the last two decades has slowed down and even reversed many of the social and economic gains which countries, especially those of the developing world, had achieved up to the early 1970s. In some cases, this negative trend has been aggravated by the very measures introduced since the 1980s to stabilise and adjust national economies. After a decade of criticisms of the negative impacts of Structural Adjustment Programmes, the shortcomings of these reforms are now recognised even by their initiators and supporters (World Bank 1989). There is evidence that the problems have been particularly acute for the most vulnerable groups in society, the very poor, women, and children (Cornia at al 1987).

Economic reforms based on liberalisation and deregulation have led, in many countries, to an increase in employment opportunities, particularly in the export manufacturing sector, either in large factories or, more often, in small-scale firms to which work is sub-contracted.[3] A large proportion of employees are female, often young migrants. This is the case in countries as diverse as Indonesia, Mexico, Malaysia, Mauritius, and Sri Lanka. This innovation can give women unprecedented chances for independent earnings, improve their skills and mobility, and expose them to enriching new environments and experiences.

However, the 'new consensus' on the positive consequences of women's employment, is being questioned. Paid work is carried out in addition to the domestic tasks for which women, worldwide, are responsible. The care of children and other members of the household, and housework, are particularly onerous where the facilities – for example, water and sanitation, but also other forms of support in education and health – available are scarce and dwindling. Another fact which challenges the consensus is that women's increased participation in paid employment may be a forced reaction to structural reforms which have led to a reduction in wages and employment, especially in the public sector, and to higher food prices. The resulting fall in real incomes makes it necessary for more women to enter the labour force, and to do so at younger and older ages than they would have under normal circumstances (Elson 1991).

Much of the new employment generated by the globalisation of the economy is poorly paid and carried out in highly exploitative conditions, against which there is little protection, because workers' organisations are being eroded or suppressed (Vickers 1991:23). Work is often of a temporary, casual type, and consequently without the health, safety, and social security benefits which more stable employment may ensure.

> *The most distinctive feature of women's labour market participation has been their take up of jobs and careers which offer part-time and other flexible work arrangements.*
> Report of the UK to the UN Fourth World Conference on Women, Beijing 1995:52.

An increase in 'flexible' and casual work for women has also become common in the West. In the UK, for example, women account for 70 per cent of home-based workers, the number of which has at least doubled between 1981 and 1993. In addition, 44 per cent of women of working age are employed part-time (the proportion in 1979 was 38 per cent). According to official sources,

These working arrangements may be attractive to some women at certain stages of their life-cycle, for example, mothers of young children may find part-time work more convenient. However, flexible and casual jobs tend to be very badly paid, and unprotected by social and safety legislation. In addition, they may severely limit women's long-term career prospects.

In other countries structural reforms have had an even more dramatic impact on women's employment. The transformation from command economies to market-dominated ones which has taken place in the countries of Eastern and Central Europe since the 1980s has been momentous, and is having consequences at every level of society. Before the transition, such countries were characterised by the very

Factory in the Free Trade Zone, Montego Bay, Jamaica, making T-shirts for Northern markets. Most of the workers are women in their twenties.

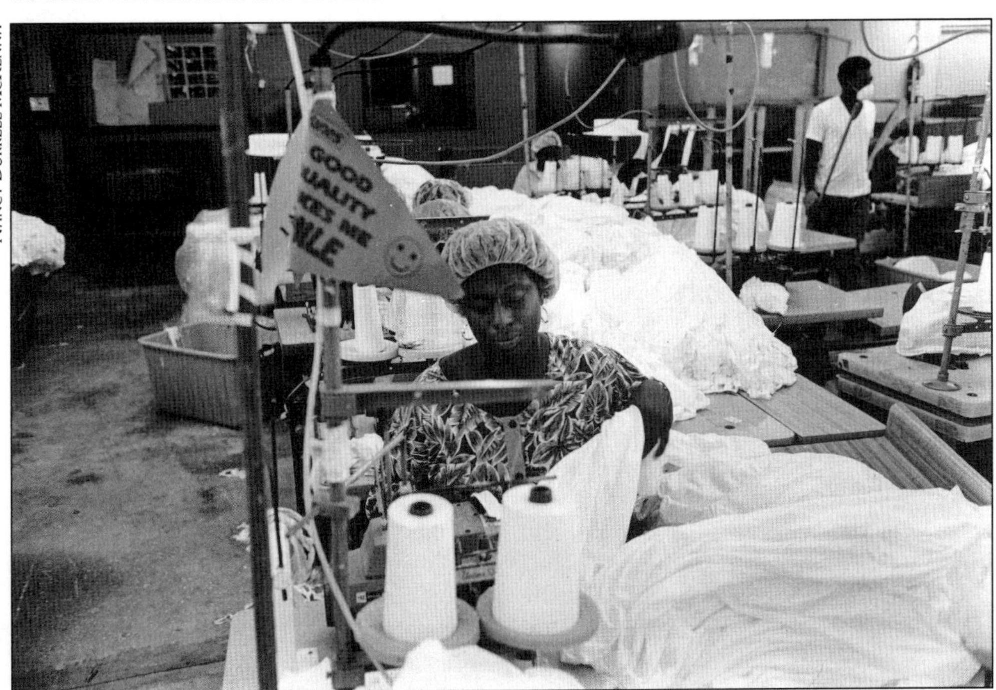

Nancy Durrell McKenna

large numbers of women in full-time employment. However, women workers did not necessarily enjoy the same benefits as their male counterparts. There is evidence of patterns of work segregation, wage differentials, and unequal career opportunities (Rimashevskaia 1992). It seems that it is the characteristics of women's employment in pre-transition times – the high cost of their maternity and other benefits, their regional and sectoral concentration – which help to explain the 'feminisation of unemployment' which has been growing across the region. By 1992 women constituted 70 per cent of the unemployed in Russia, 67 per cent in the Federal Germany, 62 per cent both in Bulgaria and in Poland (Einhorn 1993:129).

In the context of vanishing state benefits, unemployment for women implies not only a deterioration in their living standards, but also an increase in their dependence on husband or family; a loss of autonomy as well as security. This situation is exacerbated by the disappearance of the previously widespread childcare facilities for workers, and by the fact that there is little planning to overcome such problems in the long term, for example through re-training schemes (Einhorn 1993).

The type of work available to women has other long-term consequences. Casual and marginal occupations do not grant women the prestige which more secure and formal employment would give, and as a result do little to change the lack of recognition and respect that women receive in their economic role, from members of their communities and policy makers.

We have also seen that the need to work can affect a woman's educational chances and her health, hence her future well-being. This has consequences for future generations, since it has been amply demonstrated that mothers' levels of health and education are closely related to children's survival and quality of life (World Bank 1993).

Women are attempting to overcome this prevailing insecurity. There are many examples: across the newly industrialised countries the participation of female workers in unions and other labour activities is growing (Foo and Lim 1989; Lockhead 1988). The demands of such workers are often for improvements to wages and working conditions, but there are also attempts to protect their long-term interests and security as workers. Even some of those in casual and 'flexible' jobs are organising in ways which are important not only for the direct gains which can result but because they represent the emergence of new organisational forms, for example, international networking (Rowbotham and Mitter 1994).

Political insecurity

Another major cause of increasing insecurity is that familiar patterns of global alliances have been destroyed by momentous political transformations, which have led to very fluid international and regional situations in the 1990s. A particularly acute manifestation of this is the intensification of violence in regions of unresolved disputes, and the emergence of new foci of armed struggles, of ethnic and of civil conflict. In parts of the former Yugoslavia and Soviet Union, as well as in other areas, such as the Middle East, Angola, Sudan, and East Timor, insecurity takes on a violent, life-threatening form. The social, economic and personal costs of armed conflict are extremely high (Agerbak 1991:154), and are geographically spread by the fact that those caught up in such conflicts are often forced to abandon their homes and join the growing numbers of refugee and displaced people.

Full participation in political activities enhances security, because it ensures the recognition and representation of one's interests at the highest level. There is a great deal of variety in the way women share in political life, as citizens, public officials, and leaders. However, when compared to men, women's participation, especially in positions of authority and decision making, is undeniably more limited. In 1989, 79 countries of the world had no women ministers, 58 had fewer than 10 per cent, and only 22 more than 10 per cent (from Tomasevski 1993:10).

Women's difficulty in fully participating in political life has long been considered both a symptom and a cause of their subordination. Their absence from high public office is attributed to both attitudinal and structural obstacles (Beijing Draft Platform for Action, January 1995). Women's domestic responsibilities, which limit their mobility and their availability, represent a major obstacle to participation in the political and public arena.

This situation may become more acute in conditions of rapid and radical social transformations. In recent years, Structural Adjustment Programmes have increasingly contained elements of political reforms, as part of the conditions imposed on borrowing countries. The thinking behind this conditionality is that where States become more responsive and accountable to their citizens, they will be more efficient in administering economic reforms (Landell-Mills 1992). This belief is based on the assumption that all groups in society have an equal voice, which disregards the fact that women experience considerable difficulties in exercising their political rights and opportunities, and thus are not likely to benefit greatly from democratisation processes.

Developments in Eastern and Central Europe demonstrate that embarking on the road to Western-style democracy does not automatically result in enhanced political say. While women held at least one-third of seats in state socialist parliaments (Einhorn 1993:151), their representation has fallen markedly with the transition to democracy. At the first Bulgarian parliamentary elections only 8.5 per cent of the seats were won by women (Petrova 1993). The very limited number of women elected to the Federal and Czech and Slovach parliaments is said to be cause for embarrassment (Heitlinger 1993). In Rumania, the percentage of women representatives fell from 34.4 in 1985, to 5.5 at the 1990 elections (Einhorn 1993: 151). This situation has led the scholar Slavenka Drakulic to state that 'new male democracies are emerging' in Eastern Europe (cited in Eisenstein 1994:9)

Though female representatives in high office may not necessarily champion women's interests, their diminishing numbers must be seen at least as a symptom of a deterioration in women's capacity to enter the sphere of public life. Furthermore, according to Nzomo (1993:8), when women are represented in sufficiently large numbers in political decision-making, their sheer presence may influence the dominant male political culture and thus pave the way to tackle issues of gender equity and social justice, including violence against women and the provision of childcare. The slogan 'the personal is political' might have been initially a rallying cry of women's organisations in the West, but it is now one to which their counterparts in developing countries readily subscribe.

There are other ways in which structural changes, particularly those of a very dramatic nature, may undermine women's security by affecting their political participation. One of the major causes of current insecurity is the renewal of regional and ethnic conflicts which has followed the break up of established patterns of global political alliances and spheres of influence. Current conflicts differ from previous ones in the use of systematic violence against civilian populations, and the entire fabric of social relations (Summerfield 1991:159). Even in the absence of open conflict, tension and confusion characterise the political situation in many countries, especially where the state has totally disintegrated as a centre of authority and control. Under these conditions, women's hope of progress towards a more equal and effective participation in political processes is bound to be severely limited. When nationalist and other civil struggles are accompanied or fuelled by religious fundamentalism, women's capacity to retain or strengthen their political voice is threatened even more.

It is undeniable that women in most societies still have limited opportunities to contribute to political processes, and that these have either not been expanded or have been curtailed by recent structural changes. In the words of Nzumo:

> *... there is also the danger that the noble principles of democracy, freedom, equity and social justice can be abused to serve narrow interests of small hegemonic groups at the expense of the majority. Women historically have fallen victims of this kind of manipulation and misapplication of democracy.*
> Nzumo 1993:14.

However, the extent of women's political engagement and its effectiveness can be underestimated. Although women in most societies are poorly represented in senior public offices, they are often capable of influencing political processes in indirect ways, either through exercising influence over male leaders, or through their membership in organisations which, though apparently marginal and informal, may in fact play a considerable role in shaping political decisions and events (Hirschman 1991). In many African countries, for example, women's associations as diverse as informal saving groups and professional bodies are not only sources of reciprocal support and thus of social security, but can act as political pressure groups (Lachenmann 1993).

In addition, more formal and autonomous women's organisations exist which have long provided a forum for the expression of women's determination to achieve public participation. To give just a few examples: in the English-speaking Caribbean region, the 1970s and 1980s saw a revival of women's organisations, consolidated with the formation of the Caribbean Women's Association. Later, a stronger feminist perspective emerged among such organisations, especially networking and research organisations such as CAFRA, the Caribbean Association for Feminist Research and Action, and WAND, the Women and Development Unit at the University of West Indies (Tang Nain 1993). In India, women's organisations are very numerous and have been developing since the 1960s. They vary from organisations such as SEWA, the Self-Employed Women's Association, which since 1972 has been providing a range of financial and other facilities for women vendors, to centres such as Saheli, which try to establish links among women by interpreting feminist ideas through traditional values (Kumar 1989).

In East and Central Europe, the emergence of autonomous organisations is proving to be a slow and difficult matter. However, there are signs that, despite the widespread antipathy to feminism (Einhorn1993:193), this is beginning to happen. In Russia women are getting together in their professional and personal capacities, and in some cases they are explicitly committed to reclaiming their legitimate place in the public sphere (Pilkington 1992). Similarly, in the Czech Republic, dozens of women's organisations have emerged, though beset by many problems (Heitlinger 1993).

It should be clear from the above that women as *women* – rather than as workers or members of other social categories – are seeking to create forms of organisation which satisfy immediate practical needs, provide support, and thus foster their present and future security.

Social and personal insecurity

It is not only general living conditions which have become more insecure. In many cases, 'social security' institutions are experiencing crises and upheavals which may undermine their ability to perform their functions. Here the term 'social security' is not used in the narrow sense of state welfare state provisions, but as defined by Drèze and Sen (1989:16), who perceive it as an objective which is pursued through a variety of public and private means. People find security in many institutions: the household, community, trade, religious, and charitable organisations; and most notably the State.

Households represent the first line of defence against the consequences of a collapse in security, but are directly affected by recent reforms and upheavals. Break up of marriages and escalating domestic violence (Tirado 1993:105) may be symptoms of the increased tension within households. At a more formal level, community and charitable non-governmental organisations may represent a considerable source of support. However, the current growth in the demands made on them may be beyond their resources and capabilities.

Because of the increased insecurity in the economic and political fields, women's social and personal security, too, is under increased threat. The most immediate aspect of this is the widespread physical and sexual violence which threatens women's well-being and, sometimes, their very survival. Violence against women is considered the most widespread of human rights abuses (Kerr 1993:4), but it is not a new phenomenon. It has been said that 'the most dangerous place for women, the world over, is at home' (Mosse 1993:59). Social transformations seem to be responsible for the escalation of domestic violence; for example, in Fiji, the rise in marital violence is attributed to shortage of money associated with deteriorating economic conditions (Emberson-Bain 1994). Violence by husbands and fathers may be a reaction to their wive's and daughter's attempts to achieve financial autonomy. In Bangladesh, there are indications that women's easier access to loans through the activities of the Grameen Bank is leading to a worsening of domestic violence (cited by Anne-Marie Goetz of IDS, Sussex University, in a lecture given at the London School of Economics, 1994).

Women suffer from violence as part of more general conflict, and the persecution of minority groups. In the civil war in Papua New Guinea, for example, women have suffered systematic rape by soldiers (Emberson-Bain 1993); and the same brutal and demeaning treatment is experienced by women in most areas of conflict, from Bosnia, to Kuwait, Rwanda, Peru, and East Timor (Amnesty International 1995).

All forms of gender-related violence, from wife beating to genital mutilation, have severe and long-lasting effects on women's health, and on their present and long-term well-being. But violence is not the only cause of the chronic and acute health problems women experience. While problems associated with reproduction have long represented a specific and often neglected threat to women's health, there are other health risks which can be linked to recent structural changes: economic insecurity often forces women, and children, into prostitution (Mitter 1994) and this exposes them to a variety of severe health risks, from AIDS to violence.

Another threat to security is in the ecological sphere, in the deterioration of the natural resources essential for human survival. Environmental deterioration also has an impact on women's health. The effects of inadequate sanitation and water supply, and of the pollutants emitted by biomass fuels, are especially serious for women, since they perform the tasks associated with their use.

It is important not to underestimate the inter-generational impact of all of these problems. This is true both for the direct effects of the relationship between the health of mothers and that of their children, and the indirect effects that experiences of violence and abuse have on the mental and physical health of children.

Change in the role of the state

Some of the most dramatic challenges are faced by the state as an institution. Many of the reforms implemented under structural adjustment programmes contain an element of reduction in state structures and functions. In some cases, these reforms are based on an ideology which regards state 'institutions as inefficient, unresponsive to the needs of citizens, and inherently corrupt'(Macklntosh 1992). The requirement to streamline state institutions and reduce expenditures has led to the privatisation of services, and the introduction of fees and targeting of interventions, especially in the education and health sector. The consequences of such measures for social welfare have been amply documented.

Where state reforms are part of a larger set of transformations, as is the case for the Eastern European countries in transition, the implications for security are more wide ranging. This is because old systems of state responsiveness to the need of citizens, based on centralised planning and provisioning, have given way to a civil society in which people are inexperienced in seeking accountability and transparency from their elected rulers.

The crisis of the state threatens the loss of instruments, for example of law and order, necessary to protect women's personal safety; and a decline in state capacity to provide services to safeguard women's long-term welfare, through education, health and other forms of social security. In many post-transition countries of eastern Europe, for example Hungary, the social provisions on which women could count for security as workers and mothers have been severely eroded; in most developing countries which have embraced structural adjustment reforms, it is the social sector which has most severely been reduced, forcing women to make up for the shortfall (Baker 1994).

The growth of women's organisations can be understood as representing either spontaneous or planned responses, on the part of women, to 'fill the gaps' left by this erosion in state capacities, and supplement the little which is left.

Conclusions

Change and insecurity affect the lives of individuals, households, and communities in the context of recent global transformations. Women are especially exposed to threats posed by insecurity. I have tried to show that women are active in trying to ensure a degree of security for themselves and their dependants. In some cases, these strategies are spontaneous and individual, in others they rely on the organisational capacity and inventiveness that women have been developing at different levels.

What I believe has emerged from these considerations is that, while the causes of insecurity are multiple, the crisis of the state exacerbates its effects. This is not to imply that the state, its institutions and its officials, always act with full awareness of and respect for women's needs and aspirations. On the contrary, as Elson states:

The state frequently plays a major role in perpetuating social, economic and ideological processes that subordinate women
Elson, 1991:42[4]

However, the recent economic, political and social upheavals have often compromised the state's ability to perform even its minimal functions of protecting its citizens from direct threats to their physical integrity and survival, and providing the services and facilities which guarantee long-term stability and security.

Given the global nature of many of the structural transformations taking place, solutions to the problems must be found at international and regional level. This is particularly clear in the case of environmental threats, certain types of conflicts, and macro economic policies.

At the same time, at least part of the answer to increasing insecurity must lie with the state. The state can create an enabling environment for the efforts women are making to safeguard and enhance their chances, not only for survival but also security. These efforts can only give long-lasting results if they are recognised and supported by established institutions capable of providing the necessary resources.Thus responsive, and genuinely accountable governments should be counted, together with women's autonomous organisations and international agencies, among the main actors in the quest for security.

Ines Smyth is a lecturer and researcher at the Development Studies Institute, London School of Economics, on gender and development.

Notes

1 Insecurity in this paper is understood as a precariousness of current living conditions, and a threat to those of the future.

2 According to the critics, women have been left out of this notion of security as a consequence of the fact that such approaches rely on the distinction between the public, a male domain, and the private, where women are relegated (Grant 1991).

3 It is reported that the use of sub-contracting is increasing under structural adjustment (Evers 1994:123).

4 We should add here, in relation to the earlier discussion on violence, that state power is often responsible for the worst acts of individual or collective brutality against women.

References

Agerbak L (1991) 'Breaking the cycle of violence: doing development in situations of conflict' in *Development in Practice* l:3.

Amnesty International (1995) *Human Rights are Women's Rights*, Amnesty International Publications, London.

Baker E (Ed) (1994)*The Strategic Silence: Gender and Economic Policy*, Zed Books London.

Beijing Draft Platform for Action, January 1995.

Burgess R and Stern N (1991) 'Social security in developing countries: what, why and how?' in Ahmad E, Drèze J, Hill J and Sen A (Eds) *Social Security in Developing Countries* Clarendon Press, Oxford.

Cornia G, Jolly R and Stewart F (Eds) (1987) *Adjustment with a Human Face* Oxford University Press, Oxford.

De Groot (1991) 'Conceptions and misconceptions: the historical and cultural context of discussions on women and development' in Afshar H (Ed) *Women, Development and Survival in the Third World*, Longman, London.

Drèze J and Sen A (1991) 'Public action for social security: foundation and strategy' in Ahmad E, et al, op. cit.

Einhorn B (1993) *Cinderella Goes to Market* Verso, London.

Eisenstein Z (1994) *The Colour of Gender: Reimaging Democracy*, University of California Press, Berkeley.

Elson D (1991) 'Structural adjustment: its effect on women' in Wallace T and March C (Eds) *Changing Perceptions*, Oxfam.

Emberson-Bain A (1994) 'Mining development in the Pacific: are we sustaining the unsustainable?' in Harcourt W (Ed) *Feminist Perspectives on Sustainable Development* Zed Books, London.

Evers B (1994) 'Gender bias and macro-economic policy: methodological comments from the Indonesian example' in Baker (ed) op cit.

Foo G and Lim L (1989) 'Poverty, ideology and women export factory workers in South East Asia' in Afshar H, Agarwal B (Eds) *Women, Poverty and Ideology in Asia* Macmillan Press, London.

Grant R (1991) 'The sources of gender bias in international relations theory' in *Gender and International Relations* Grant R and Newland K (Eds) Routledge.

Heitlinger A (1993) 'The impact of the transition to communism on the status of women in the Czech and Slovak Republics' in Funk N and Mueller M (eds) *Gender Politics and Post-Communism* Routledge, London.

Hirschmann D (1991) 'Women and political participation in Africa: broadening the scope of research' in *World Development* 19:12.

Kerr J 'The context and the goal' in Kerr J (Ed) *Ours by Right* Zed Books, London.

Kumar R (1989) 'Contemporary Indian feminism' in *Feminist Review* 33 Autumn.

Lachenmann G (1993) 'Informal social security in Africa from a gender perspective' paper presented at the International Workshop on 'Insecurity in the 1990s: Gender and Social Policy in an International Perspective', LSE, April.

Landell-Mills P (1992) 'Governance, cultural change and empowerment' in *The Journal of Modern African Studies* 30: 4.

Lochead (1988) 'Retrenchment in a Malaysian Free Trade Zone' in Heyzer N (Ed) *Daughter in Industry* APDC, Kuala Lumpur.

Macklntosh M (1992) 'Questioning the State' in Wuyts M, Macklntosh M and Hewitt T (Eds) *Development Policy and Public Action* Oxford University Press, Oxford.

Mitter S (1994) 'On organizing women in casualised work' in Rowbotham S and Mitter S (eds) *Dignity and Daily Bread: New Forms of Economic Organizing among Poor Women in the Third World and the First* Routledge London.

Mosse J C (1993) *Half the World, Half a Chance,* Oxfam.

Nzomo M (1993) 'Engendering democratization in Kenya: a political perspective in democratic change in Africa: women's perspective in Mukabi-Kabira W, J Adhiambo-Odul and Nzomo M (Eds) *Association of African Women for Research and Development,* ACTS Gender Institute, Nairobi, Kenya.

Petrova D (1993) 'The winding road to emancipation in Bulgaria' in Funk N and Mueller M *op cit.*

Pilkington H (1992) 'Whose space is it anyway? Youth, gender and civil society in the Soviet Union' in Rai S, Pilkington and Phizacklea A *Women in the Face of Change* Routledge, London.

Report of the UK to the UN Fourth World Conference on Women, Beijing 1995.

Rimshevskaia N (1992) 'Perestroika and the status of women in the Soviet Union' in Rai S, Pilkington and Phizacklea A, op cit.

Rowbotham S and Mitter S (1994) *Dignity and Daily Bread: New Forms of Economic Organizing among Poor Women in the Third World and the First* Routledge London.

Summerfield D (1991) 'The psychological effects of conflict in the Third World' in *Development in Practice* l: 3.

Tang Nain G (1993) 'The retreat of the state in the English-speaking Caribbean: its impact on women and their responses', paper presented at the International Workshop on 'Insecurity in the 1990s: Gender and Social Policy in an International Perspective', LSE April.

Tickner J A (1992) *Gender in International Relations* Columbia University Press, New York.

Tirado S (1993) 'Weaving dreams, constructing realities: the Nineteenth of September National Union of Garment Workers' in Mexico' in Rowbotham S and Mitter S (Eds) op cit.

Tomasevski K (1993) *Women and Human Rights,* Zed Books, London.

Smyth I, Saptari R and Maspyati (1994) 'Flexible specialization and small-scale industries: an Indonesian case study' ILO, 22-21 WEP 234.

Vickers J (1991) *Women and the World Economic Crises,* Zed Books Ltd, London.

World Bank (1993) *World Development Report 1993: Investing in Health: World Development Indicators,* Oxford University Press.

Women, war and transition

Judy El-Bushra and Cécile Mukarubuga

War represents transition in its most violent and bewildering form. Yet the destructive capacity of war derives not from physical violence alone but also from the deep injuries to people's sense of themselves and their sense of identity as a member of a community. In war, both the physical and the moral underpinnings of society are brought into question. In the long term they may be either strengthened or weakened, with consequences for women, men, and gender relations within that society.

Any attempt to generalise about war is bound to demean the experiences of individuals caught up in it. It is over-simplistic to assume, for example, that men are necessarily the perpetrators of war while women are its peace-loving victims. In reality, men and women may each be protagonists of war in various ways, and are dramatically affected by it, both physically and emotionally.

However, the inadequacy of the international response to the various conflicts which have occurred during the 1980s and 1990s requires us to deepen our analysis of how and why wars take place and are resolved, and the implications of this for the international community. Much new thinking is needed, to attempt to construct new models from unfolding realities and to search for new insights, rather than adhere to stereotypes.

In the majority of conflict situations, it is men of the 15-50 age group who, willingly or unwillingly, tend to be actively engaged in fighting; while women, with older males and children, attempt to maintain the integrity of the household and community in whatever way they can. It is largely women who take on the role of shielding families and communities from the shocks, stresses, and disruptions of unstable change. When that change gathers pace and turns into the turmoil of war, women's capacity to carry out this 'buttress' role is constrained by the stresses that they themselves come under during conflict, creating tensions not only for women themselves, but also for the whole society (El Bushra and Piza Lopez, 1994).

This article explores these tensions, first through examining some points common to most armed conflict, and secondly by focusing on Rwandan women's experience. Following this, some critical questions will be raised about the challenges which these issues raise for the international relief and development community at large.

Conflict and power relations

Both gender roles and conflict relate fundamentally to the exercise of power. Conflict distorts gender roles, creating tensions between the different demands placed on women. Though women's role in protecting and maintaining the family is magnified in war, to the extent that they may take over many of men's functions, they mostly retain their subordinate position in power structures. Many communities stricken by conflict, and heavily dependent on women to maintain production and generate income, still retain the male domination of organisations which control economic resources, such as committees to oversee the distribution of relief goods. Many of the 'predatory formations' in which individual power-seekers control war economies based on illicit trade (in drugs, arms, or stolen food aid, for example) depend on women acting as retailers or in other support capacities (Stott, 1990). If the disempowerment of women were to be successfully addressed, would this have an impact on the incidence or the conduct of war?

How can women support and protect their families, and maintain some semblance of community cohesion, when they are in need of support themselves? Women's role in assuring household food supplies requires them to go outside the home (to work in fields, to collect rations, to sell produce) and this exposes them to risks of physical injury (for example, the majority of victims of landmine injuries are women and children). The need to develop economic coping mechanisms brings to the fore women's skills in the management of household resources, but may also force them to engage in activities such as prostitution or illicit trade in drugs and alcohol which place a long-term question-mark over their future social acceptance (El-Bushra and Piza Lopez, 1994). Women have a role in protecting children, the sick, and other women who are particularly vulnerable through age or pregnancy, yet this role makes them less mobile and increases their own vulnerability.

Rape in conflict

In armed conflict, there is a widespread practice of targeting women for particular abuse, precisely because of their association with the identity and well-being of their community. The use of rape and other forms of sexual humiliation as a weapon of war has been documented most recently in ex-Yugoslavia, but as a strategy is as old as war itself (Brownmiller, 1975). It hardly needs to be emphasised that rape may have serious physical and psychological effects on women, which may last the rest of their lives. Women who have been raped or forcibly abducted and 'married' by their captors (recent examples where this strategy has been used systematically include Uganda and Mozambique) may never be able to return to their previous lives (Bennett et al, 1995; McGreal, 1993). The impact of the pregnancies that result from rape is massively damaging. Estimates of rape pregnancies in warfare include, for example, 20-50,000 Bosnian women in 1993 (Vulliamy, 1993) and around 5,000 women in Rwanda in 1994 (Mukambuga, personal observation). The future for children born as a result of rape is uncertain: their mothers may be emotionally and materially unable to care for them, and, unlike almost any other children, they may become a huge unwanted charge on the community.

Women as symbols of social identity

When external pressures on a society increase, a common reaction is to uphold women's 'virtue' as a vital element of cultural identity, and thus to try to protect and to control this virtue. The tendency towards fundamentalist interpretations of religion often has to be understood as a response to the threat of cultural erosion. In France, during the second world war, women who were believed to have fraternised with the occupying German army were humiliated in public by having their heads shaved: in Somalia, women seen talking to American soldiers during 'Operation Restore Hope' were stripped naked and beaten (Maier, 1993).

Psycho-social effects of conflict

The impact of war on the psychological health of individuals and communities is complex and not fully understood. Clearly, psychological stress results from witnessing shocking events. But profound stress might also arise from unresolvable tensions between a person's view of themselves on the one hand, and on the other, the self which events oblige him or her to be. If women are forced to resort to socially unacceptable activities, are submitted to humiliating and abusive treatment, or fail to protect their children, the damage to their self-esteem may result in lifelong emotional impairment (Bennett et al, 1993).

Women's long-term ability to maintain and protect the integrity of their communities is threatened by the psychological impact of their experiences during conflict. Coming to 'understand' the political causes of conflict can reduce psychological stress, as can support from social networks of individuals who have been through similar experiences (Zur, 1993).

Women and reconstruction

Finally, is there also a potential conflict between women's role in assuring cultural continuity on the one hand and the eventual need for reconciliation and peace? Handing on to future generations the sense of identity and the knowledge that goes with it is often an important role for women. Yet it may also involve informing those generations of the historical reasons for the conflict, and perhaps thereby keeping it alive (Cock, 1989).

It is within women's power to reconstruct or reinforce relationships and attitudes across generations, by the way they bring their children up. In many instances it is women who decide at what moment hostilities have gone too far, exert pressure on men to stop fighting (often by withholding sexual services), or create dialogue with estranged neighbours. Although women are not the only peacemakers, it is often they who build the peace, often in private and 'from the bottom up', unacknowledged and unsupported (Ferris, 1992).

The case of Rwanda

In extreme situations, the impact of war is so destructive that the capacity to cope, physically and emotionally, is put in question. Rwanda may provide an example of this (for all information in this section see ACORD, 1995). In certain parts of the country as much as 80 per cent of the population is now estimated to be female. This proportion is maintained in the new generation as well (boys were targeted during the massacres just as deliberately as men), which clearly has long-term significance for the nation as a whole as well as for individual families.

Before the outbreak of genocide in 1994, Rwandan women had been fighting hard against structural problems such as food shortages and economic and environmental constraints. The legal framework was becoming more positive towards women, and though women were becoming freer in their movements, husbands still controlled resources and owned all the property of the family. There were some improvements taking place, however, and women were very active in associations and in the informal sector, seeking out any activity which could generate an income. Women's occupancy of political posts was minimal, mainly because of low educational levels. However, women's groups and associa-

ANNE MACKINTOSH

Refugees in Rwanda.

tions were beginning to acquire a certain political weight and negotiating strength.

The tragic events in Rwanda left a large number of widows and their children deeply traumatised. Women have undergone every sort of humiliation: rape leading sometimes to pregnancy (many girls have already given birth to children who resulted from rape); loss of husband or children (especiallyboys); rape of small girls in the presence of their mothers; voluntary or forced participation in massacres. Today women find themselves deprived of everything – their families, friends, possessions – and without emotional or physical strength to rebuild their lives.

Women on their own have to exercise both their own functions and those previously exercised by their deceased husbands, for which nothing had prepared them. Women who lack skills to take up new roles previously exercised by men may well be forced into polygamous relationships in which their rights may be compromised. Many heads of families are young adolescents, women without experience and without support, and for whom prostitution offers a source of material support.

Many women have large families (including numerous orphans) to maintain, yet face the problem that both production and productivity have been affected by lack of labour. Many women are without shelter or clothes and even without food, while prices on local markets are unattainable. Yet there are no opportunities for salaried work or funds to start up income-generating activities. Moreover, the majority are traumatised by the horrors they have seen and lived through; this includes both the victims and the perpetrators of genocide. The massacres of 1994 have led to a breakdown in intercommunal relations in which mistrust between neighbours has become the norm. Many women live in fear and uncertainty about the future, especially those who are living in isolation, their neighbours having been killed or living in exile. Others are afraid of militias returning, and others again fear to live in the place where they have seen their families perish.

The issue of women's legal rights (for example to access to cultivable land, to family possessions or property) has become critical in post-war Rwanda. Though current laws are supportive of women's claims, most women lack the knowledge or support to make them, and similarly find it hard to lodge complaints of rape or theft.

Coping in the aftermath

Most Rwandans have experienced profoundly terrible events. But to assume that they are incapacitated by shock would be to deny human adaptability and the instinct for survival. Some women have now begun to form groups along the lines of pre-war associations, to help one another with agricultural production, to build houses, and to start up savings and credit schemes to finance income-generating activities. To deal with their psychological stress, some are in the habit of meeting in the evenings to give each other the courage 'to face the night'. In these meetings they express the horrors that they have lived through, which otherwise they would not dare to talk about.

Dependence on women in present-day Rwanda is high, so high in fact that some of the constraints hitherto faced by Rwandan women are beginning to fade. In the past, for example, women rarely owned land and had almost no control over the products of their own agricultural labour. Now, however, such restrictions are inappropriate, given the imperative of a rapid return to economic productivity. Whether this represents a fundamental shift in the legal entitlements of women, or merely a temporary arrangement to assure food security, remains to be seen.

Critical questions

The example of Rwanda illustrates some of the ways in which this extreme dependence on women can call into question their capacity at both personal, household and community levels, to meet the demands placed on them by their situation. Yet it also illustrates that the 'needs' of these women go well beyond food aid and other forms of relief, to encompass, amongst other things, shelter and personal security for themselves and their families, mutual support to cope with the psychological impact of traumatic events, the establishment and maintenance of women's economic and legal rights, and the opportunity to gain a livelihood. Examples such as this pose a critical challenge to the international aid community: how effective can it be in meeting these needs in conflict-related emergencies, and hence in reducing future shocks for the communities affected? Is there a contradiction between the need for continuity and the need for change?

Conflict provides opportunities for change in social relationships including gender relations. Rwanda provides an example of how turbulent situations can oblige men and women to reassess their own and each other's roles, setting aside old preconceptions and stereotypes in favour of more rational and just relationships. Post-conflict reconciliation and reconstruction likewise offers the opportunity to acknowledge the contributions and sacrifices made by different groups of people during the war. If this means that women's roles both inside and outside the domestic arena are acknowledged and validated, and that new areas of responsibility can be carved out by them, change will be positive. Whatever women suffer during war, many gain such self-confidence, self-respect, and autonomy in the process that they resolve never to slip back into the old ways, when they were beholden to men and lacked the skills to make their capacities and feelings known.

However, it is often not clear in practice how far changes in gender relations that occur as a response to conflict are really fundamental: they may be only temporary changes, to be suppressed again when the war is over, or they may be merely superficial. If gender relations appear to change as a result of conflict, is this merely a more efficient reordering of the factors which consign women to a role as carers and protectors within the private sphere, or does it reflect a genuine reassessment of women's and men's complementary rights?

In Europe, 50 years after the end of the second world war, and in spite of unprecedented opportunities for women in terms of education, control over reproductive health, and legal equality, women have still not found a way to redress their subordinate status. In the new economic turbulence of the 1990s – for example, in the widely emerging pattern of male unemployment and female semi-employment – women are still seen as responsible for family maintenance, by taking responsibility both for household economic survival and for the care and socialisation of children, and in this process also maintain cultural continuity. Yet as before, they do so without having significant power of decision-making or control over resources, at either the domestic or the national level. By standing for continuity, stability, identity, and reconciliation in times of chaos, are women setting out a new and more elevated position for themselves, or are they simply restricting themselves to the same old stereotypes?

How can the international community best support women and men in dealing with turbulent change?

Ultimately, the relationship between women and men in any society is the business of the individuals themselves. Humanitarian agencies have the responsibility to ensure that their actions do not aggravate women's subordinate position, something which can often result from even the best-intentioned interventions if proper monitoring is not carried out. They also have the capacity to act positively by being facilitators in the debate between men and women on the kind of social relationships to be put in place. Ironically, conflict situations may provide an opportunity for this debate to take place. Both emergency and post-conflict rehabilitation programmes must therefore assist women and men to find a new accommodation within their changed circumstances, enabling the society concerned to progress.

Promoting discussion on gender relations within the community, as opposed to within their own staff or partner organisations, remains a considerable challenge for development organisations, yet when carried out skilfully it appears to be associated with significant improvements in women's condition and status, and may result in permanent changes in attitude and behaviour (Hadjipateras, 1995). Incorporating such dialogue into the activities of agencies assisting in conflict emergencies may at first sight appear incongruous in the face of people's priority needs for shelter, water, and food. Yet it may take only small adjustments in methodology to ensure that agencies consult with both men and women before they commence activities, and the act of consultation itself is a means of initiating dialogue.

How can the international community support women more effectively in situations of conflict?

In wartime, individuals each play a part in shielding others and the community from shock. In doing this, they are contributing to the long-term survival and health of the society from which they gain their identity. To the extent that men and women have different gender roles, the ways in which they do this will differ. Men will tend to be preoccupied with externals, such as waging war, diplomacy, and politics, protection of dependents, leadership, and mobilisation; while women will probably see their contribution as being within the household and the local community, and in the transmission of values to their children.

The ability of different individuals to take on a stabilising role depends on how they themselves cope with the changes that are going on around them. This in turn is affected by the changes that are happening to their society and how far it has the material, political, and psychological capacity to keep itself from fragmenting. The individual and the society are thus intertwined, and the integrity and stability of one can be shattered more easily if the other is also under pressure.

How can international relief and development agencies strengthen the capacity of societies to resist the strains imposed by conflict?

This is a critical question for agencies, as it implies the possibility that through their assistance they may have actually reduced this capacity. To what extent has the international aid community focused its attention on women and tailored its assistance to meet their particular needs? Unfortunately, few regard this question as being sufficiently important even to warrant collecting the necessary information. The operation of the 'contract culture' in the field of emergency relief has led many international agencies to see themselves as accountable to their paymasters (mostly Western governments, and in terms of the provision of quantities of supplies), rather than to the communities they serve; and even those who have attempted to move beyond this perspective have not looked much further than male community leaders.

In conclusion, women's needs and rights must be taken into account in relief efforts, and this cannot be done by using male power structures. Much work is needed on identifying forms of organisation and mutual support which have meaning for women, and working out ways of enhancing their capacity.

This involves developing an understanding of what women do to maintain, protect, and plan for the future of their families, and the support they can call on from within the community, both in material and in psychological or emotional terms; and of what constraints exist for them, both within and outside the community. Women's rights must be recognised and strengthened both locally and in the practices of the humanitarian agencies themselves, and in international law and conventions. Rebuilding the long-term future must begin at the same moment as the provision of relief supplies; in designing programmes of emergency assistance agencies should adopt an approach that values research and dialogue and the capacity to understand how the community functions 'from the inside'. Above all, women's role in maintaining the fabric of community interaction must be recognised, alongside their potential to promote reconciliation and peace education, and this potential be given the chance to flourish at the right moment.

Judy El-Bushra is ACORD's gender officer, responsible for institutionalising its gender appproach. Her particular interests are promoting gender training at field level and research on gender and conflict issues.

Cécile Mukarubuga, previously ACORD's East Africa Gender Officer, is now Regional Representative for East Africa. She is focusing on re-establishing ACORD's programme in Rwanda.

References

ACORD (1995) 'Programme de réhabilitation en faveur des femmes seules à Kigali, Rwanda' (mimeo).

Bennett O, Bexley J, and Warnock K (eds) (1995) *Arms to Fight, Arms to Protect*, Panos, London.

Brownmiller S, 1975, *Against our Will: Men, Women and Rrape*

Cock J, 1989, 'Keeping the home fires burning: militarisation and the politics of gender in South Africa' in *Review of African Political Economy* 45/46

El-Bushra J and Piza Lopez E, 1994, *Development in Conflict: The Gender Dimension*, Oxfam UK/I

Ferris E (1992) *Women, War, and Peace: An Issue Paper*, Life and Peace Institute, Uppsala.

Hadjipateras A (1995) 'Gender review: interim report,' ACORD, (mimeo).

Maier K 'Women fall victim to Somalia's prejudice', *Independent* 5.1.93.

McGreal C 'Renamo conceals child "brides" of boy soldiers', *Guardian* 11.6.93.

Stott L, 1990, *Women and the Armed Struggle for Independence in Zimbabwe*

Zur, J (1993) 'The psycho-social effects of "La Violencia" on widows of El-Quiché, Guatemala', *Focus on Gender* 1:2.

Algerian women and political choice

a time of transition

Imane Hayet

Currently, Algerian women are facing a major crisis. In a complex and changing political environment, the status of women is at stake, threatened by conservative forces associated with Islam, which are likely to win in Algeria's forthcoming multi-party elections. How are women involving themselves in politics to determine the course of the election?

In 1989, after the coming of the multi-party system and freedom of association, the feminist movement in Algeria became legal. Its objective was to fight for women's rights, and their opportunity for employment, and against the obstacles to women's education; and to improve the status of women within the family, especially given the huge inequality brought about by the family code adopted in 1984.

The transition to democracy in Algeria has suffered, and continues to suffer, from ambiguities in the nationalist approach to the demands of 'modernity' along Western lines, and the place of Islam and universal law in the move towards this modernity. The discussion continuously swings between the two extremes of secular values, and religious dogma and tradition. In many respects, women stand symbolically at the centre, between these forces, and it is they who suffer most from the tensions between them.

The question of political choice for Algerian women today is inseparable from the question of democracy and the problems of achieving it; it is also bound up with the question of equality between men and women, which is less an issue of the public sphere than of the private domain. In exploring these issues, I will draw on the results of a survey I undertook in 1994 using a representative sample of the population (833 women, and 466 men).

Democratisation and the growth of civil society

Democratisation in Algeria has encountered problems because of the state of development of society. Illiteracy is widespread (notably among women), and the quality of the educational system has fallen. Other problems include demography, high unemployment, the lack of a strong civil society to mediate socially and politically, and the spread of vote-catching practices. Before the move towards the democratic regime in 1989, individual men and women played only a notional role in the political framework of Algerian life. Having been marginalised from power for so long, the establishment of a parliamentary democracy has 'opened up a horizon where the individuals of yesteryear without authority, the *amma* (the people) closely followed by women, [have become] major partners in the political game (for power)' (Mernissi, 1990). In 1989, after 30 years of a single-party system during which no form of autonomous expression was permitted, hundreds of non-governmental organisations (NGOs) mushroomed. In 1992, there were around 3,000 registered organisations.

Women's organisations have increased in number, but less so than others. The women's movement in Algeria is recent; it can be traced back only ten years. Women's associations focusing on welfare and cultural activities, which are often led by militants from the Islamist movement, are much more numerous than those working on women's rights. Most women's organisations are involved in social work, such as training girls in manual work, handicrafts or clerical work, or in welfare work with girls who cannot cover the costs of their marriages. However, there are now a few organisations interested in issues directly related to women's status, such as the Association for the Defence of Oppressed Women. These organisations have been to a large extent inspired by the democratic movement, or more precisely, by women who were closely associated with the liberal opposition parties which existed before the coming of the multi-party system and before the emergence of the Islamist parties.

This embryonic 'feminist' movement started having its own public gatherings when these were still forbidden, at the end of the 1970s. The movement mainly revolved around the issue of the 'family codes', which had been discussed since the 1970s and were adopted only in 1984, because of the resistance to them. The movement is opposing these codes in the name of the principle of equality between the sexes enshrined in the Algerian constitution, as well as the principles of the Universal Declaration of Human Rights. However, none of Algeria's women's organisations is working directly on the issue of political participation of women.

Women's demands to use their own votes

In 1990, the victory of the Islamic Salvation Front (FIS)[1] during the Municipal Elections shook the feminist movement. In 1991, just before the Legislative Elections, the movement reacted by rallying together to lobby for the cancellation of votes by proxy. It was successful in this, despite the opposition of the General Assembly and the extremist parties; it was helped by the tacit support of an element of the powers-that-be. The automatic delegation to the husband or father of a woman's right to vote was annulled, even though the electors were leading to victory an Islamic fundamentalist party, which emphasises the importance of Islam in political and social life, and one of whose credos is denial of equality between the sexes. Men had been authorised to vote on behalf of their wives since 1970, and the practice was extended to all female members of the family, particularly in rural and semi-rural areas, where women rarely go to the local government offices.

The feminist movement in Algeria thus has not had to fight for the right to vote, since this has been recognised in all State Constitutions since independence, but to demand that the law should apply equally to men and women in the exercise of this right. The feminist slogan was 'A vote is like a prayer, no one can do it for you.' The demand met with indifference on the part of many women, who expressed only lukewarm support.

Women's demand to use their own right to vote was refused by the National Assembly influenced by militant sections of the party in power, the National Liberation Front (FLN),[2] and Islamic Fundamentalist parties and associations. The ground given for opposing this electoral reform was 'respect for tradition'. The reform was finally introduced in 1991: it does not cancel the 'automatic' right of proxy given to the husband, but requires him to legalise it by asking his wife to confirm her agreement in writing to the local authorities.

This reform cannot be said to have been just the result of pressure by the feminist movement; the reform was adopted because of the effect on the government of women's votes in the elections. The government was frightened of seeing itself doubly sanctioned by the wives and sisters of Islamic Fundamentalist male electors authorised to vote for them within the old law, and this fear certainly played no small part in the government's decision. However, the publicity around the reform allowed the women's movement to bring the wider issue of equality between the sexes into the political arena. This was a subject on which the government and parties had been discreet throughout their campaign.

Women's involvement in political life

In our survey, the rate of abstention among women was notably higher than that among men in the two democratic elections. The first round – the Legislative Elections of 1991 – showed 30 per cent abstention, for which women accounted for three-quarters. The majority of these were poorly educated or illiterate women, and particularly housewives (*El-Watan*, 1992).

As regards other forms of political involvement (demonstrations, strikes, conferences, meetings, local committees, collective action committees, membership of associations, and political discussions) our enquiry showed that few women took part in such activities: there was a large difference between men and women. The low level of involvement of women must be seen in relation to the nature of the activities.

Why was women's political participation in the two elections at such a low level? The novelty of having a pluralist, democratic election may be one explanation; less than a decade ago, such elections would have been inconceivable. An additional explanation may be that it is conservative values which stop women becoming involved; they are doubly excluded from political activities by the fact that they take place in the public domain, and that decisions are taken. Other results confirmed this, showing that women with a dogmatic attachment to religion tend not to become involved. It was the youngest women (those aged between 20 and 29 years), and women with the best education, who were most often involved in political activities.

Women and the 'Islamic model' of society

The research examined women's and men's support for a conservative way of life, supported by fundamentalist political forces. Are women or men most in favour of an 'Islamic model' of society?[3] Almost twice as many men than women supported the idea of an Islamic society: 44 per cent of men placed themselves at the highest level of the scale of 'support for some aspects of the model of Islamic society', compared with 23 per cent of women.

However, it would appear that the difference in opinion as regards a model of Islamic society depends not only on sex, but strongly depends on the level of education. Sympathy for the model decreased as the level of education rose. There was a noticeable difference between those who had gone on to secondary or higher education, and the rest (20 per cent of the highest-educated considered themselves to be very close to this model, compared with 39 per cent of illiterates and 31 per cent of those of medium or technical level). This result was the same for men and for women.

From this, I would conclude that, because of the precariousness of their status in society and the awareness of it which they acquire from experiences in private and public, women sense to a varying extent the threats which an Islamic society would pose to the condition of women, and to the few rights they have painfully acquired. Women who are educated or who work present a challenge to the dominant traditions on the role of women; this group is particularly aware of these threats. The notion of the irreversibility of acquired rights is certainly a matter which causes tension between the sexes; this tension then finds its expression in the difference between men and women in their support for the Islamic model.

Women's aspirations to equality: the Sharia laws

In the research, questions were asked on the opinions of Algerian women (and men) about granting rights denied by the current family code based on the *Sharia* [Islamic law]. We constructed a scale[4] to measure the aspirations for emancipation in regard to the laws of the *Sharia*. Among individuals who most favoured this emancipation, there were no less than 67 per cent women, compared with 20 per cent men.

However, this apparent aspiration for emancipation did not seem to be connected to lack of sympathy for religious practices (namely prayer, fasting and abstaining from alcohol). This suggests that respondents do not necessarily question religion and religious practices in themselves, but question the 'public' character of religious norms (Addi, 1993), which constrain behaviour. These social constraints are seen as discriminatory. The desire for emancipation from the laws of the Sharia can therefore be interpreted as evidence that women are no longer viewing certain religious norms as sacred – particularly those norms which closely affect their private life.

This would explain another finding: that women who are most against these laws are not the highest educated, since the latter have more ways of escape from social constraints imposed by religious norms, because of the higher social status they have acquired through their education.

Women's political sympathies

We asked whether women who wish to retain or to acquire rights which are questioned by the *Sharia*, necessarily turn towards political organisations. This is not the case. There was widespread indifference to politics. Nearly 40 per cent said that they were not interested in politics, or that no party matched their aspirations, or did not reply (15 per cent).

There may be two reasons for this lack of interest in politics, and more particularly in political pluralism. First, women commonly see politics, particularly a multi-party system, as likely to give rise to conflict. Women's status in society means that they are ill-equipped for survival in conflict, and they are therefore more anxious about it than are men; in line with this, when women in the survey were asked about ways of improving the situation in Algeria, they, more than male respondents, emphasised 'understanding', 'fraternity', 'peace', and 'compassion'.

The second, related reason for women's lack of interest in politics relates to the link which they may be making between the birth of the pluralist political parties in Algeria and the widespread violence and terrorism which followed this. After 30 years of single-party rule, the period of real freedom of speech and action lasted for only two years – 1990 and 1991 – before terrorism erupted. This has caused 30,000 deaths, and has completely compromised the development of the women's movement, especially the part which is situated outside the Islamicist movement.

To those with only limited understanding of politics, the partisan system may appear to be the main 'cause' of the terrorism.

The women's movement has splintered on political lines since legalisation, and this has led to a great loss of support. A lack of material and financial resources narrows further the abilities of the women's movement, the priorities for the state being elsewhere. Grassroots work has been neglected, and the movement has not succeeded in mobilising women around concrete issues. The discussion of politics has seemed to overwhelm a wider debate about women's marginalisation in all areas of life. This has alienated many women, particularly young women, for whom the pluralistic system is still new and intimidating. In addition, the emergence of religious extremism, and its attack on the image of the liberated Westernised woman, both ideologically and through physical violence and intimidation, alienates women who feel that this view of feminism will penalise the legitimacy and the work of these associations which had already become weakened.

Women's favoured political parties

It seems from this research that the social choice regarding whether or not one supports equality between the sexes, as represented by support for a political party, is less dependent on social factors than on sex. In support of this, of the 60 per cent of female respondents who preferred one political party, 45 per cent favoured the democratic parties, 21 per cent favoured the National Liberation Front (the previous single party), and 15 per cent favoured the Islamic Fundamentalist parties. A further 19 per cent had political sympathies which combined two or three of the major political groups.

In contrast, male respondents were divided into two: sympathisers with the democratic parties, and sympathisers with the Islamic Fundamentalist parties. More women than men supported the democratic parties and the FLN, while more men than women supported the Islamic Fundamentalist parties.

The way forward: the Presidential Elections

The date of the forthcoming Presidential Elections has yet to be announced. Preparations are being made in a context of continuing violence, and the formation of new political alliances between some of the democratic parties (for example, the Socialist Forces Front and the Workers' Party), Islamic Fundamentalist Parties (FIS and Nahda), and the previous sole party, the National Liberation Front.

Will women be able to make a clear cut choice? It is to be feared that the government's lack of transparency about the political implications of multi-partyism, allied to the low level of political understanding among women, will result in the majority of women oscillating between two electoral choices: the first being to abstain, and the second being a 'non-partisan' choice of the government candidate. The 'understanding', 'union', 'fraternity', 'unity', 'return to peace and security' and 'to put an end to terrorism', which women most frequently propose as one or more conditions for ending the crisis in the country, makes the government (and its candidate) the ideal representative of these aspirations, if one dismisses the possibility of voting for its direct competitor, the Islamic Salvation Front.

Of course, these hypotheses on the electoral behaviour of women at these new decisive elections are dependent on the outcome of the present negotiations between the Government and the FIS (and the Armed Groups which it controls), the response of the other Islamic Fundamentalist and democratic parties, and degree of freedom given to the means of expression and information.

Already some *députés* in the provisional parliament (*Conseil National de Transition*) are proposing amending the Article of the electoral law concerned with the 'proxy' vote, and replacing it with the previous 'automatic' vote where the husband simply has to present the *livret de famille* [family record book] – the aim being, they reason, to increase the level of participation! If such an amendment were accepted, the 'formal' abstention rate for women could effectively be lower than in the previous legislative elections, but would we then still be able to speak of, or measure, the participation or abstention of women?

With the increase in violence and terrorism since 1992, women and feminist associations are threatened. Their activities are hindered, and many feminist militants go underground when they are unable to leave the country. However, they continue to fight for civil peace and democracy, to denounce violence and murders, and to fight against extremism. It is due to their initiative that many demonstrations have been organised against violence and for democracy in the last four years.

Imane Hayef, of the University of Algiers, is a member of Collectif Egalité Maghreb 95, and has researched extensively into the situation of women in Algeria and the Maghreb.

Notes

1 The FLN was legalised in 1989 and later formally dissolved in 1992, by the Algiers Court of Appeal.

2 From Independence until 1989, the FLN was the only legal party in Algeria, and has been the ruling party from Independence to date

3 This scale (the Gutman Scale) was constructed from the questions concerned with: the freedom of women to wear or not wear the *hidjab*; the construction of a 'true Islamic society'; meeting with future husbands before marriage; total Arabisation; the implementation of limits for women's rights; the application of the Sharia law.

4 This scale was constructed from questions concerning: the granting of guardianship of children of divorced women; the equal division of inheritance between daughters and sons; the suppression of polygamy; the exercising of a professional activity by mothers.

References

Addi, L, *L'Algérie et la démocratie*, La Découverte, Paris, 1994.

El-Watan (an independent Algerian daily), *Sondage post-électoral* undertaken a few months after stopping the second round of theDecember 1991 legislative elections, Algiers, October 1992.

Mernissi, F, *Les sultanes oubliées*, Le Fennec, Casablanca, 1990.

Women's political participation

Mozambique's democratic transition

Ruth Jacobson

In October 1994, elections were held in Mozambique for a President and a National Assembly. This article focuses on the civic education programme which formed a background to the elections. Much of the civic education material dealt with gender issues, but this was in a way which failed to acknowledge the structural aspect of women's subordination and the possibilities of sanctions against women's political participation.

The 1994 elections were the first in Mozambique to be held on the 'one person, one vote', multi-party pattern which is associated with political structures in the West. It was the hope of virtually all Mozambicans that these elections would provide a means to close a terrible chapter of war and instability in the country's history. They were seen as representing Mozambique's 'transition to democracy', in the wider context of the historical shifts within the Southern African region.

However, there are some important reservations to be made when we consider the gender elements in this transition. All too often, complex social institutions and processes involving women as well as men are described in universalised terms. So one encounters 'the' family, 'the' farmer or, as in this case, 'the' Mozambican voter, with no differentiation. When I made a tour of voting stations in and around the capital city of Maputo at the start of the first day of voting, and talked to women and men in the queues, I found a restrained but positive anticipation. Nationally, the turnout of voters was very high, with women represented in proportion to their majority position in the adult population. What brought these women to stand for hours in order to vote? What did 'democracy' mean for them? To help to answer this, the Norwegian government's aid organisation, NORAD, commissioned me to produce a study of the entire electoral process. This article draws on that study,

While there was no formal exclusion of women from the electoral process, the structure of gender relations in Mozambique, combined with specific conditions around the political process, placed fundamental obstacles in the way of their full and equal participation, as voters and as participants in the institutions which ran the election. This suggests that claims for a 'transition to democracy' must be looked at carefully, and always be contextualised with reference to the historical circumstances of the countries concerned, rather than seen as a process which remains unchanged regardless of its context.

The context

In the lead-up to the elections, Mozambique's history of exploitation and conflict stimulated complex debates concerning sovereignty and 'ownership' of the political process. During the course of my research, Mozambican women frequently referred to having to 'squeeze' themselves into a suit of ready-made clothes, imported from the West. They were emphatically not rejecting 'democracy', but wanted considerably more space and time to develop their own priorities.

After Mozambique achieved independence from Portugal in 1975, the liberation movement, Frelimo, converted itself to a Marxist-Leninist political party, and the country became a one-party state, based on a state socialist model of centralised power, state control, and large-scale solutions. During the first six years of Independence, there were significant achievements: the infant mortality rate was cut by half, and the national primary health care system became a model for the World Health Organisation. Primary school enrolments tripled, and illiteracy rates dropped, according to the 1980 Census. These advances were not matched in the economic arena, where the grandiose plans for economic development failed to materialise, while the peasant farming section was almost totally neglected (Hanlon, 1984). Today, the principal means of livelihood continues to be agriculture. The 1991/2 survey estimated that 90 per cent of all women in the active population work in agriculture, mainly as family farmers.

Although weak economically, independent and black-ruled Mozambique constituted a political threat to South Africa, and hence became the main object of the apartheid regime's destabilisation policy. In 1980, South African Military Intelligence took over the training, arming, and management of a force which was to become the Resistencia Nacional Mocambicana, or Renamo. The ensuing war was devastating: more than 1 million people were killed (7 per cent of the population); more than 4 million people were made refugees inside or outside the country; and more than US$20,000 million in damage was done, with massive destruction of bridges, railways, health posts, and schools.

This led to the collapse of the Mozambican economy, and also brought about fundamental changes in Frelimo's position. Mozambique became one of the most aid-dependent countries in the world. Since 1987, at the behest of the World Bank and the International Monetary Fund (IMF), a Structural Adjustment Programme (SAP) has been imposed, involving the acceptance of a market economy and associated features, including lifting of price controls, removals of food subsidies, and introduction of user charges for health services, and cuts in public spending (Abrahamsson and Nilsson, 1993).

Frelimo renounced its position as the sole legal political party and incorporated multi-partyism into the new Constitution of 1990. The protracted peace negotiations with Renamo, which concluded in the Rome Accord of 1992, stipulated the direct election of the President and of delegates to a national legislative body on the basis of a secret and universal vote.

Voter registration

The conditions under which Mozambicans became members of the electorate were laid down in the 1992 General Peace Accord and the 1993 Electoral Law. The body responsible for this process was the Commissao Nacional de Eleicoes (National Electoral Commission – CNE). Each province had its own CNE, responsible for administering the national programme. The identifying symbol of the CNE, particularly important in a non-literate context, was the figure of a woman wearing traditional dress, with a baby on her back, against the rising sun. This was to serve a two-fold purpose: first, to stress the importance of women's involvement, and secondly to represent the 're-birth' of Mozambique (interview, CNE spokesperson).

All citizens could vote if they were aged over 18, not serving a criminal sentence, and 'of sound mind'. The final figure for registered voters was 6.396 million (81 per cent of the population). In the absence of gender-disaggregated figures for voter registration, observation of the registration process suggests that women did turn up to register in numbers which reflected the overall demographic balance.

However, women's participation in the organisations which oversaw this process was not representative: only two of the 21 members of the CNE were women. Registration teams had a minority of women in virtually all areas, and many teams contained one woman, or none at all. Educational requirements for membership of the teams discriminated against women; whereas Mozambican enrolment rates at the start of the educational system are not noticeably biased, by the sixth year there are major differences between the achievements and participation of boys and girls, especially in the rural areas. In 1990, the illiteracy rate was 55 per cent for men and 79 per cent for women. Women are further excluded from the public sphere by their inability to speak the official language, Portuguese. In 1991, women represented 75 per cent of the rural population aged 20-24 who could not speak Portuguese, and 80 per cent of the urban population (SIDA Country Gender Analysis, 1993). This might have been countered if the CNE had decided to promote actively the recruitment of women who had 'equivalent' qualifications – for example, women who had considerable organisational experience through their work with community organisations.

Educating the voters

Educacao Civica was the term given to the variety of programmes that were mounted during the pre-election period. The English translation of 'civic education' does not fully convey its full range, which went from step-by-step demonstrations of how to vote, to long speeches on the history and significance of democracy and human rights. The 'core' of civic education incorporated the implications of multi-partyism; voting as a fundamental right; the act of voting as an individual act of free choice; the secrecy of the ballot; and a practical section on the actual process of voting.

Among the bodies involved in funding, training and implementation were the CNE itself and its associates including the United Nations Development Programme (UNDP), the Association of Western European Parliamentarians (AWEPA), religious communities, aid agencies, including several of the major bodies operating in Mozambique such as USAID, Western organisations linked to specific political movements or autonomous promoters of democracy, and Mozambican non-governmental organisations (NGOs).

Among the last category, women's organisations of various types were crucial for the success of the civic education programme, because their existing community-based structures provided a way of reaching the non-literate sectors of the urban and rural populations. The leading organisation in this area was the Organisacao das Mulheres Mocambicans (OMM). This had formerly been the Frelimo party's mass organisation for women but was now operating as an NGO.

Other, smaller women's organisation were also involved and developed their own distinctive material. For example, in a *bairro* [shanty-town] of Maputo, a group of women put together a participative role play that was relevant to their own positions within the community, as heads of their own households.

Women's organisations involved in civic education frequently found themselves marginalised in terms of resources. Transport for teams around the rural districts was often unavailable. This was one reason for the uneven and inadequate coverage of the civic education programme as a whole. While women were highly visible in some areas, such as the OMM teams, they were noticeably absent from other organisations.

Expectations, accountability and transparency

Civic education stressed that legitimate political power comes through the existence of a multi-party system and the possibility of choice; it was much less specific about the issue of *permanent* accountability, sometimes implying that the act of voting was in itself sufficient guarantee of democracy.

Some at least of the responsibility for this must lie with those organisations from the North which were heavily committed to promoting multi-partyism, without taking into account existing concepts of legitimacy and accountability within Mozambican culture. Their materials and training sessions were distinctly lacking in transparency about the constraints and deficiencies of the democratic system as actually practised in the Western industrialised countries. Mozambicans were rarely, if ever, informed that in many Western countries the turnout for even a national election is often around 60 per cent and sometimes under 50 per cent. When asked to estimate the percentage of female members of parliament in Britain, most guessed at 50 per cent and were startled to learn that it is actually only 12 per cent (as at the last election in 1992). The impression that many of the external agencies had given of the functioning of democracy had led them to assume that issues such as gender inequities must have been resolved by the women of the North!

Gender issues in civic education

A variety of media were used to get the information across, including radio, theatre, print media, and television. There was obviously the intention to maximise the participation of women in the process, but this has to be assessed in terms of the implementation of this objective. Much of the terminology used in print media was formal and inaccessible even to the very small proportion of the female population literate in Portuguese. Although efforts were made to reach non-literate women through other means, such as radio and theatre groups, they were of limited impact. As a result, one could frequently encounter women who, when asked if they had registered, would proudly produce their card, with their photograph on it, but who were not clear as to its purpose. In many cases, it was regarded as a new form of identity document, or even as a ration card. (However, this kind of confusion was by no means confined to women.)

In the coverage of multi-partyism and of universal suffrage, there was a formal emphasis on the inclusion of women. The more complex issues of gender-specific constraints were tackled by some organisations. For example, the training manuals produced by AWEPA, which were widely used, included separate material on Women and Democracy. The manual uses the story of a Mozambican woman, Ana, to illustrate fundamental principles of human and women's rights, of the peace process, and of multi-party democracy. It points to the vital role that women play in Mozambican society, despite which they still experience discrimination in the home, at work, and in political life. This material had the advantage of being directly relevant to the lives and concerns of many women, both as trainers and as recipients of civic education. It also drew on their knowledge of collective organisation.

However, in the main, the underlying

structural aspects of gender-based power relationships within the family, which affect women's ability to participate in political and other activity in the public sphere, were not addressed. Where they were, for example in the story of Ana, the complexity and depth of the obstacles to women's participation may have been minimised. Ana decides, at the urging of her women friends, to let her name go forward as a candidate for the legislative assembly. Her husband remonstrates with her, saying that he can take care of political matters for both of them – doesn't she trust him? She replies that yes, she does, but

...some things in this country have to change. Women's lives are very hard. And I want to do something. I know a lot about the problems of women, and they have confidence in me.

The couple continue talking about this, and in the end, her husband accepts that Ana is right:

All right. Now let's organise our life in a different way; I am going to take care of the problem of getting wood [for cooking] every day, and our son is already old enough to go to the market to sell our produce. This way, we can divide up the work in our family a bit better and you can have the time for your political work. But don't forget that you have a family and a husband!

Most women saw this scenario as an unrealistic ideal rather than commensurate with their own experience of strongly entrenched gender differences within the family; these were not so easily transformed by rational discussion.

Gender issues were not only addressed by women's organisations. For example, at a work-place session run by a team from the Mozambican trade union movement, with an almost entirely male audience, there was this appeal:

You know, we men don't usually talk about things with our wives, or our children. But now, with this new time in our nation's history, we've got to start doing this, we've got to make a new way of doing things in our families .... So please, when you go home, don't just keep all that we have done today to yourself, tell your wife about it, answer her questions so she will know what to do on election day.

The secret ballot

A consistent theme in civic education was the need to reassure people that their vote would be secret, need not be divulged to anyone, and could not be 'seen' by anyone, whatever their status in the community. Belief in what may broadly be called supernatural forces is deeply rooted throughout Mozambique, though rarely officially acknowledged. A crucial distinction is made between the power to heal possessed by the *curandeiro* and the power to do harm of the *feiticeiro*. These forces are also associated with the power of divination, through consulting the ancestors. They may all be merged in the one person who is, of course, known to his or her local community. The notion of a secret ballot, crucial to the Western model, cannot incorporate these beliefs, which were sometimes expressed in the process of civic education such terms as: 'Surely, I do not have to put my [ballot] paper into the same place as the *curandeiro*...' or 'I don't want to have to put my hand in the same place [the ballot booth]...'

In the public debate, women were frequently presented as more likely to be influenced by fears of witchcraft, on the basis of their lower level of formal education and involvement with the 'modern' world. This stereotype does not acknowledge the degree to which men, even those with urban, industrial jobs, continue to believe in and consult *curandeiros* and *feiticeiros*. It also underestimated the extent to which women, already experienced in community organisation, were in a better position to take on the message of civic education than men, who did not have access to those information networks.

The civic education practitioners attempted to counter these fears by stressing the way in which the voting process would be monitored and supervised by election officials and international observers. This approach was consistent with the 'rational' Western model but could not really hope to resolve anxieties linked to a different conceptual framework. Some of the CNE's material engaged with the problem in a more light-hearted way. A television campaign showed a smartly-suited man consulting a diviner in order to know the result of the election; the diviner throws the bones several times, looking more and more puzzled and finally admits that even he can't give an answer because 'the vote is secret – even to the ancestors!'

Women as a voter category

It cannot be emphasised too strongly that the women of Mozambique, as in any other country, are not a single, homogeneous category. The economic interests of urban women traders are not the same as those of peasant farmers; there are also major differences related to religion and ethnicity. For example, women in the matrilineal societies of northern Mozambique were highly critical of the way in which the previous Frelimo government had marginalised older women who had formerly held important ritual and ceremonial positions. One of the negative aspects of making exaggerated claims for 'democratic transition' is that it makes it more difficult to engage with these differences. This has implications for women's organisations which need to identify those areas where there *are* shared interests.

The election itself

The CNE calculated that close to 90 per cent of those entitled to vote had done so. The election was certified as 'free and fair' by the UN, despite acknowledged disruptions and irregularities. Reports from all over the country suggested that women turned out in force to vote; a 'spot check' on Maputo polling stations certainly confirmed that they formed the majority of the voters. On the first day of voting, all voters had long waits, often up to six or seven hours. The Electoral Law laid down categories of special priority voters, which included pregnant women, but under the pressure of numbers on the first day of voting such priorities were not always observed. At one station young men were seen clamouring successfully to be let in to vote before other people, including the elderly. On the other hand, it was also noted that, on occasion, women with children at the breast were sometimes given priority, leading to instances of 'baby-swapping' in queues.

Civic education had included simulations of what would happen on voting day, with the civic education teams playing the part of election officials and the audience able to go through a 'trial run' using mock ballot papers and boxes. These exercises served to diffuse some of the anxieties felt by many people around the procedures. However, there were numerous reports of people appearing quite bewildered, and needing help from the election officials. The Presidential ballot paper contained the photographs, names and parties of candidates. The legislative paper had the names of the 14 parties and their symbols. Civic education had stressed the need for illiterate voters to memorise the photographs and symbols, but there was still a strong possibility of confusion and uncertainty. Media coverage almost invariably referred to this in terms of 'confused elderly women', as if elderly men were not also affected.

The marginalisation of women within the CNE continued at polling, in terms of the gender balance of the polling station staff. It was rare to find a female Presiding Officer; women were employed usually in the less important positions. Among the *delegados de lista* (accredited party representatives who had important duties of observation and verification), only 10 per cent were women (personal communication), even in parties with relatively high numbers of female candidates.

Voting for a better future?

The Presidential election was a clear victory for the Frelimo candidate, Joaquim Chissano, with 53.3 per cent of the votes as against Renamo's 33.7 per cent. There was a much closer outcome in the National Assembly vote. As for the representation of women, the percentage of women in the Mozambican legislature is now 24.4 per cent; Frelimo had adopted a one-third quota system for women candidates, so that 48 of their 129 political representatives are women, selected in a secret ballot system. Renamo rejected this policy, and had far fewer women candidates; they have 12 women deputies out of 112. Not surprisingly, there were no female Presidential candidates.

The election campaign was characterised by the absence of real political content. For example, regarding the issues of health and education, both parties promised large-scale improvement, without acknowledging the constraints on public spending which the World Bank and IMF would demand of any new government. Neither addressed one of the most fundamental problems affecting the health and education sectors. The levels of pay for teachers and health service workers are so low that employees are forced to rely on supplementing their income by bribes and the misuse of government material. As one woman put it:

I'm pregnant, and when I go to the clinic for my check-up, I know that I have to take 5,000 matacais with me so that the nurse will see me. I don't blame her, I know that she has to do it because she has to look after her own children ... but it makes me wonder, what does all this talk about democracy and elections mean. Will it solve these problems?

The Mozambican people have shown a quite extraordinary willingness to commit themselves to reconciliation and reconstruction after a bitter war. The multi-party elections were a crucial aspect of this process, and women's role in them was vital. At the same time, women had reservations about the form and content of the transition process, which must be taken seriously if there is to be a sustainable, accountable political context for development. There will be severe external constraints on the activities of the government, as well as continuing inequality. One must hope that Mozambican women and men will have the opportunity to develop principles and practices of democracy which they feel are appropriate for their history and culture, and which allow for a new and more equitable vision of gender relations.

Ruth Jacobson is a researcher and lecturer on gender issues in politics. She is currently completing a Ph.D. on gender and citizenship in Southern Africa. Her full report on the Mozambican elections, Dancing Towards a Better Future? *can be obtained from: Department of Peace Studies, Bradford University, Bradford BD7 1DP, UK*

References

Abrahamsson H and Nilsson A (1993) *Mozambique in Transition: A Study in the History of Development during 1974-1992,* Peace and Development Institute, Gothenburg University.

Hanlon J (1984) *Mozambique: The Revolution under Fire,* Zed:London

Gender, culture and later life

a dilemma for contemporary feminism

Kasturi Sen

This article argues that current feminist perspectives, and development planners and policymakers, have failed to address the issue of ageism and the marginalisation of older women's interests and contribution to development. Aiming to contextualise women of the north and south in terms of demographic, social, and economic change, the article attempts to view women's life cycle as a celebration in struggle.

Until recently, ageing women have received little attention from the women's movement. Feminism's engagement with the multiple facets of women's lives – stressing the intertwined nature of reproduction and production – has tended to reach a cut-off point at menopause. Interest in menopause has been perfunctory, and the years after menopause have been ignored. Older women, for example, are always excluded from research into health and ill health in later life, despite their predominance in absolute and relative numbers. The lack of attention to the ways in which women's gender identity links with ageing deepens structural subordination, and reinforces traditional patriarchal stereotypes, implying that women's life cycle comes to an end between 44 and 50 years, with the loss of the natural capacity to reproduce.

This phenomenon appears to be common throughout the world and, I would argue, is especially so amongst the emerging feminist movements in many developing countries. Development agencies working on women's health issues also reflect this narrow outlook, in collusion with the dominant models of the medical world. Such a perspective is not only hostile to any woman-centred perspective on health, but renders older women invisible as a group.

Demographic change

In 1950 there were about 200 million people over the age of 60 years in the world, evenly distributed between developed and developing countries. By 1975 this had increased to 350 million elderly people, with a similar distribution. However, current estimates strongly suggest a definite change in this pattern by the year 2000. Elderly people living in developing countries will constitute over two-thirds of the total and in 2025 their share will have increased in absolute terms to 72 per cent of the global total (United Nations 1991).

According to the UN, between 1950 and 2025 the world's older population will have increased by a factor of six, which is in effect double compared with the total world population, which will increase by a factor of three. The distribution of elderly people will also have changed: by 2025, in absolute numbers, 84 per cent of older people will be living in developing countries. These proportions will vary considerably between countries in accordance with the pace of demographic transition. In some countries, such as Kenya or Nigeria, elderly people might form only 8-9 per cent of the total population but in others such as India or China, might rise to 15 per cent by the year 2025.

The process of demographic transition – declining rates of fertility and a corresponding increase in life expectancy – took place over a period of a century in many of the countries of northern Europe. In developing countries, improvements in public health, nutrition and to some degree the availability of medical technology (particularly in the form of contraceptives, however negative their implementation and long-term health consequences) have brought similar changes but over a much shorter space of time. However, the issue of coming decades will not be the numbers per se but the contributions of older people to the development process (Kinsella et al 1993, UN 1991)

Table 1: Percentage increase in elderly populations 1990-2025, Developed and developing countries

Country	% increase
UK	35
Sweden	33
Denmark	47
Germany	66
Indonesia	414
Malaysia	321
Brazil	255
China	220

(Compiled from Kinsella and Tauber *An Ageing World II*, International Population Reports, The US Bureau of Census.)

Gender and longevity

While there are considerable variations between countries on the levels of life expectancy, in virtually all countries of the world women outlive men.There are both social and biological reasons for such longevity. The main point to be made here is that consequently, sex differences in absolute increments are most apparent at the oldest ages, where women predominate. This is highlighted by Table 2.

Table 2 Life expectancy and gender gap in selected countries worldwide

	Life expectancy men	Life expectancy women	Gender gap
Sweden	73	79	4
Australia	71	78	7
Soviet Union	64	74	10
China	62	66	4
Japan	73	79	4
Philippines	59	62	3
Indonesia	49	51	3
India	46	45	-1
Egypt	54	56	2
Mauritania	41	44	3
Guinea Bissau	39	43	4
Ethiopia	38	41	3

Note: In India, unlike any other country listed, average female life expectancy at birth is less than that of males.
Life Expectancy at Birth: the average number of years a person may expect to live.
Gender Gap: the difference in years between female and male life expectancy.
(Source *UN Demographic Yearbook*, From: *The New State of the World Atlas*, Kidron and Segal 1987, New York.)

It can be seen that women out-survive men in most regions and countries of the world. Currently in the developed world, differential mortality favours women at all ages especially at the oldest ages (over 80 years). In Europe, for example, one in four women were over 60 years of age compared to one in seven men. The situation varies in different parts of the world. In the NIC countries such as Hongkong, Korea, and Uruguay, gender differences are similar to those of Europe and North America. In parts of South Asia, (notably India), the inverse would apply due to an excess of female mortality during early childhood and during the reproductive period.

Both developed and developing countries have been experiencing changes in the structure and composition of their populations; life expectancy continues to rise throughout the world, with women on average surviving between 4-5 years longer than men in both developed and developing countries. In coming decades, however, the gap between male and female life expectancy is expected to decrease due to the deleterious health effects of recent global economic strategies. In the North, this differential is also closing but for different reasons: it is being suggested that women (of all social backgrounds) are emulating the health and life-style behaviours formerly associated with men, such as smoking and drinking, which in recent decades has had a disproportionate effect on male mortality.

Culture, productivity and ageism

A perspective that informs this article is a critique of how ageism has been compounded by the way in which feminist thinking of the late 1980s and 1990s seems to have placed 'culture' at the forefront of women's struggles: religious culture, the culture of violence, the culture of education, the culture of reproduction and health, and the culture of 'otherness' derived from anthropological research. The material world appears to have been replaced by a 'cultural order'. I would argue that over-emphasis on the cultural aspects of women's marginalisation obscures the material and structural basis of gender inequality, and of ageism.

In dominant capitalist economic theory, old age is perceived as a time of decrepitude and dependence, since more often than not the capacity to produce money values (that which economists would describe as 'productive output') is restricted by enforced retirement (Phillipson 1982). Just as women's contribution to production and reproduction is often invisible and uncounted, older people's contribution is also largely unrecognised. Older people are assumed to be unproductive; old age is, therefore, not celebrated as a positive part of the development process, since it is not associated with countable contributions. Contributions made by older people cannot be measured by monetary values alone, since they are often 'in kind', and thus rarely incorporated into national statistics. Consequently, old age is often viewed with fear and anxiety, as the 'age of burden'.

The universal nature of unequal power relations between men and women must mean that there cannot be an age cut-off point in feminist understanding of gender issues. The question that should be asked is whether, in ignoring the realities of the ageing process and the contribution of older women to production and reproduction, contemporary feminists are also by implication sharing the ageist perspective of market economists.

Structural Adjustment Programmes (SAPs) are an example of a structural cause of poverty where women of all ages suffer most acutely, because of the lack of recognition of their needs and of their contribution to the processes of production and reproduction. In the past decade, not only has women's workload increased but there has been a negative impact upon their health; while the bargaining power of women of all ages has been undermined. Worst of all, there is growing evidence that economic adjustment causes women's food consumption to go down, due to various factors which include the pressure to grow cash crops, the escalating cost of basic foods, and rises in the cost of public transport (Commonwealth Secretariat 1989; UNRISD 1995).

It is therefore ever more urgent that feminists do not reinforce the view of women as passive victims of cultural oppression and material forces, but instead emphasise that, however dispossessed and marginalised they may be, working-class and peasant women have a history of organising themselves to combat violence and marginalisation in creative and strategic ways. A shift in outlook by feminists, particularly with regard to older women, is essential to enable women – especially those who own few resources other than their labour and who today are increasingly and miraculously surviving in greater numbers into old age – to grow old with pride and not simply be viewed as victims of cultural oppression.

Old-age security

The nature and transformation of work in the past two decades means that older women worldwide have very limited economic security. In most countries, resources and life style in old age depend on savings from earlier incomes or the control of assets. Structural inequalities related to employment, coupled with a very narrow definition of what constitutes work which is recognised and valued in national accounts, ensures that women's work, which is largely in the 'informal' and subsistence sectors of the economies of developing countries, is uncounted, despite its critical significance to family survival. Domestic labour, which includes the essential roles of caring for other relatives and for offspring, and of reproduction, is also uncounted. In developed countries, transformations in the realm of work from core manufacturing activity to service sector operations has meant a proliferation of part-time employment where, in the past decade and a half, women's work has been located. Part-time labour rarely provides occupational cover and therefore women have to rely on a non contributory state pension which is only available in a handful of countries, and perhaps not for much longer (Sen , 1995).

Given these factors women are less able than men to accumulate sufficient savings or qualify for pensions, with the exception of a small minority of privileged women working in the informal sector. This has dramatic effects on the financial autonomy of women in later life.

In most developing countries, women are under pressure to produce male children – not solely to promote cultural vanities, but rather to ensure security in old age from the relatively better assured employment opportunities of males over females in later life. Other factors which are highly discriminatory against girl children (access to food and education, and social and sexual mobility) are a consequence not only of the prevalence of an ideology of patriarchal son-preference, but also associated with a need for security in old age, within the wider context of poverty and growing disparities between and within nations. Among the better-off families, the desire for male children may not have a material cause, but remains entwined with the patriarchal values of honour and carrying the family name. This is complementary to the perception (however ironic) that sons are a key to the provision of moral and economic security in old age. This belief holds despite the reality that the majority of carers of elderly people, across the world, are women.

Older women and health

Women's longer survival is not always associated with good health. Research on women's health in the past decade suggests that women are exposed to longer periods of chronic health conditions, such as arthritis, diabetes, and osteoporosis. Clearly this will be mediated by socio-economic status and opportunities in earlier life, but these health problems are increasingly prevalent among older women worldwide.

Older women are also likely to experience long-term reproductive complications of numerous pregnancies or unsafe abortions. The prevalence of cancer of the breast and of the cervix has been found in recent years to be higher among older women than among women of the reproductive age group. With better screening and earlier detection this trend is likely to alter, but only in those regions of the world where such facilities are available. The growing significance of women's health conditions is related to the alarming rate at which public health-care facilities worldwide are shrinking under the weight of economic reforms.

Fees and user charges, for example, are widespread, and are having a dramatic effect on the take-up of health care, especially amongst older women and poorer people generally. This phenomenon is common in both developed and developing countries, as an effect of monetarist economic reforms. Health policy makers in the coming decades will need to consider how to provide affordable health care for older people, and older women in particular, which emphasises primary health care and prevention rather than focusing on costly curative services.

Policy implications

According to the UN, the lead agency for the promotion of ageing issues, there is an urgent need for social and economic policies to meet the challenge of a growing and more active elderly population throughout the world. Ageing should be an opportunity to be utilised for the benefit of society and of older people themselves be it materially or otherwise. Empowering older people, particularly women, enhances their capacity to meet their diverse social and cultural needs. In this sense, according to the most recent International Plan of Action on Aging, developmental and humanitarian aspects of the ageing process are closely interlinked (UN 1991).

What are the policy implications of greater numbers of older women surviving? The need to view older women as key partners in the development process is essential due to the dramatic increases in life expectancy in developing countries in recent decades.

Defining old age

There are intrinsic problems in defining and classifying old age. This is because it is influenced by a range of factors, from socio-legal to economic to biological. For example, it is obvious that the meaning and experience of old age will be perceived very differently in a country such as Sierra Leone, where life expectancy in 1991 was 34 years, and a country such as Japan, where average life expectancy in the same year was 80 years. Chronological age and well-being is also affected by lifestyle. An encumbered and arduous lifestyle will inevitably hasten the onset of ageing. This is relevant not only between countries, but between rich and poor within the same country.

If a woman has spent the whole of her life engaged in arduous physical labour, suffered malnourishment or a poor diet, experienced numerous pregnancies and lactating episodes, her ageing process will be quite different from that of a woman who may have had only one or two pregnancies and a relatively comfortable life in material terms (Kalache, 1991).

NEIL COOPER

Elderly woman digging earth bunds, as part of a food-for-work scheme for drought relief, in Tigray.

Therefore, when defining old age, it is important to take into account social differences that have an impact upon biological age and the quality of later life. Policy makers and researchers have tended to use 60-65 years as a common marker for the beginning of old age, for use in cross-national comparisons of health development and ageing. Whilst this may be 'technically' appropriate it is often strongly criticised, sometimes by older women themselves, as being an arbitrary classification which does not reflect real life experiences. While in industrialised countries, this age classification is used as a marker for official retirement, many feel that the label is false; and for the majority of older people in developing countries, there is no formal departure from the labour force. In most developing countries with an economy based on agriculture, people continue to work as long as they are able; in urban settings too, older women often work as domestics, washing, cooking, selling flowers and food, and caring for children so that younger women can take up opportunities for waged work.

Counting the contribution

The increasing concern among policy makers about financial dependence in later life (World Bank, 1994) has unfortunately been driven by anxieties about the rising costs of health and social care. This has accelerated policies for user charges and private occupational pensions at a time when they may be least affordable, except for a minority of the population. It is quite clear that, given the inequalities and discrimination experienced by women worldwide, none of these facilities will be accessible for women even for current cohorts of those in mid-life who have yet to reach the official age of retirement. Even those who are ageing over the next decade, are unlikely to have access to private schemes. It is thus ever more essential to reassess the value of women's work. It could be possible, for example, to provide credits and payments for the multifarious roles women play throughout their lives. This would ensure a life with more dignity in old age, and improve relations between generations. There is growing evidence to suggest that families are increasingly unable to provide financial support for surviving parents, especially to cover the potentially high costs of health care.

In a number of countries of Latin America, Africa and Asia, some of the issues of poverty in later life are being dealt with by state sector and NGO support for income-generating activities. There has been very successful support for rural and semi-rural paid work provision for older women. This has in addition challenged some of the stereotypes of ageing as a time of decrepitude and dependence, attitudes frequently inherited from Western agencies where sex-segregated roles and formal retirement converge to provide a grim picture of women in later life.

The following description reveals perhaps a truer, though rapidly changing, world for older women where skills mattered and labour in kind was valued:

Haj iya Osaba spent her days in Nigeria doing many things. She gathered herbs and made her own medicines, treating women and children for various illnesses. She helped deliver infants, being knowledgeable in the skills of midwifery. She rented rooms in her compound. She sold henna, which the women use for cosmetic staining of their feet and heads. When the deaths of women or children occurred, she was called upon to prepare the body, supervise the organization of the deceased's estate, and carry out many of the tasks associated with the burial...

Coles, C, in *The World Ageing Situation 1991*, UN, 1992.

In today's harsh material world, such skills need to be counted and incorporated into national statistics such that the majority of the world's women may be counted as holding up more than 'half the sky', since they are the ones producing much of the goods and services which keeps the world moving. Contemporary feminists, among others, will also need to become convinced of this worth, and of the value of a women's life cycle beyond the years of reproduction.

Kasturi Sen is Associate Fellow at the Oxford Centre for Environment, Ethics and Society where she co-ordinates a programme on Health, Environment and Development for the EEC. Her book, Ageing: Debates on Demographic Transition and Social Policy *was published by Zed Books in 1994.*

References

Commonwealth Secretariat (1989) *Adjustment for the 1990s*, London.

Kalache A (1991) 'Ageing in developing countries' in Pathy M S J (ed) *Principles and Practice of Geriatric Medicine*, 2nd edition, Chichester, J Wiley & Sons.

Kinsella K and Tauber C (1993) *An Ageing World II*, US Department of Commerce, Bureau of the Census, International Population Reports, Washington.

Phillipson C (1982) *Capitalism and the Construction of Old Age*, London, Macmillan.

Sen K (forthcoming 1995) 'Health and social security in later life: a critique of current paradigms', Sunny Toyota International Centre for Economic Research and Development (STICERD) Lloyd-Sherlock P and Johnson A (eds) *Occasional Papers*, The London School of Economics and Political Science, London

United Nations (1991) *The World Ageing Situation 1991*, New York, UN.

UNRISD (1995) *Report on Adjustment and Poverty*, Copenhagen.

UNRISD (1995) *Adjustment, Globalization and Social Development*, reports of the UNRISD/UNDP International Seminar on Economic Restructuring and Social Policies, New York, 11-13 January 1995, Geneva, UNRISD.

World Bank (1994) *Averting the Old Age Crisis* Washington, World Bank.

Coping with transition through organisation

Techiman Market, Ghana

Carolyne Dennis and Ernestina Peprah

This article examines the effects of transition to a market-driven economic model, on the activities of women traders in Techiman Market, Ghana.

In the past 15 years, the experience of Ghana has been one of economic crisis followed by drastic economic restructuring through the implementation of the Economic Recovery Programme (ERP). This transition has been accompanied by a serious fall in the living standards of large sections of the population, and an increase in the reproductive burdens of women (Clark and Manuh, 1991). The objective of the ERP is to 'transform' the Ghanaian economy, and it is clear that since 1984, when it was instituted, there have been radical changes in economic and social relations in Ghana.

In these circumstances it is a challenge to attribute an appropriate 'weight' to the impact of the ERP on people's lives without implicitly comparing the Ghanaian economy to a machine which will not function until international and national policy makers pull relevant 'levers'. Present-day Ghana is also striking in the extent of external intervention in the economy through influence on the structure and processes of governance, and public administration. Multilateral agencies, bilateral agencies, and foreign NGOs are all important players at the national level and, with decentralisation, increasingly, at the local level.

Through an examination of a particular process of economic transformation in which indigenous women's organisations have played a crucial role – the expansion of the market at Techiman, a district capital in Brong-Ahafo – this article argues that the extent and depth of the market system in Ghana has led to the development of well-established traders' associations, which have played a crucial role in the current transition and the resulting expansion of Techiman market. The focus will be on those aspects of the objectives and practice of indigenous women's associations which are potentially relevant to those income-generating and credit groups established by external donors in Ghana, with a view to mitigating the impact of structural adjustment on poor women and their households.

Background

The marketing of essential food items through Techiman Market has increased phenomenally in the past ten years. In southern Ghana, as in much of West Africa, this trade is largely in the hands of women. It appears that this massive expansion in the volume of trade in foodstuffs in the market has been 'managed' by associations of women traders. This process is linked to many important issues in Ghana: the relationship between trade and agricultural production, and the contribution of such associations to civil society, for example. Our research aims to provide insights into the possible limitations of donor-funded women's income-generating groups in providing sustainable incomes to poor women in Brong Ahafo.

Techiman is now a rapidly expanding town with an estimated population of 36,785 (Spring Programme, 1989, 66). It is the administrative capital of Techiman District in Brong Ahafo Region. Techiman has, for a long time, been one of a number of important trading centres on the major routes between North and South. Since colonial times there has been a retail market on Fridays, in a weekly cycle with other similar markets in nearby small towns. In the past ten years this has become an important three-day wholesale market, especially for yams and grains, and the expectation is that in the next five years it will become a permanent market.

This very visible rise in economic activity is nearly all based on the expansion of the Techiman market. In addition to the retail market selling foodstuffs and consumer goods to the residents of the town and its surrounding communities, Techiman Market is now primarily a centre for the trading of bulk foodstuffs such as yams, plantains, cassava, and grains which are brought from the farms and bulking centres in the north of Ghana for onward transportation to major urban centres, especially Accra; and for sellers of bulk smoked fish who come from the coast. The expansion of the market is difficult to quantify but it can be indicated by its progression in a short time from one day a week, to a four-day market, and soon to a permanent market; and the fact that market fees now provide 70 per cent of District Administration revenues in Techiman.

The government of Ghana's restructuring policy on agriculture has focused mainly on the cocoa sector (Sarris and Shams, 1991). State policy towards the food trading sector has often been hostile, and the intensity of this hostility was greatest in the early 1980s (Robertson, 1983). The situation in food trading has been helped by the abolition of price controls on essential foodstuffs in 1984 which was part of the ERP. It seems likely that the most important contribution of government policy to the expansion of the Techiman Market has been the construction of the major North-South Road through the town. This improved accessibility and the dynamic local economy has led to increasing donor interest in intervention in the town.

Other contributory factors are the improvement of road transport conditions by the late 1980s and 1990s, and the growing emphasis, at household and community level, on the importance of food production and exchange after a period of food insecurity in the 1980s. This is reinforced by present economic unpredictability, inflation and continuing threats to household survival.

Women traders' organisations

The traders are organised into market associations defined by the goods they sell: yams, fish, plantain, and cassava, for example. Apart from 'male' trades, such as butchers, the traders in foodstuffs are all women. Specialist traders, whom Clark calls 'travellers' (Clark, 1994), go out to the farming areas to buy crops such as yams, cassava, and plantain, sometimes buying a future crop for credit from farmers. They bring the foodstuffs to Techiman where they are sold to wholesale traders, who then sell the goods to 'travellers' from Accra who take them to the coast. The very recent rapid expansion of the bulking side of Techiman market means that this specialised division of labour between wholesale traders and 'travellers' is likely to be less entrenched than in longer established markets such as Kumasi Central Market.

In the most widely used models of women's organisations (Moser, 1993), these traders' associations fall into the category variously identified as Commercial or Market based. One of the interesting empirical questions raised by these models is how far actual organisations correspond to them, in particular situations. As will be discussed below, the traders' associations have a wide set of objectives.

Techiman market is renowned for yam trading. Yams are a highly prized food in Ghana; they require particular skill to grow, are bulky, difficult to transport and they perish quickly in the trading process, although not as quickly as plantain and cassava. It is a specially difficult trade to enter, because of the need to establish networks of relationships with farmers and transporters. Traders also need access to up-to-date market information and substantial sources of credit or capital to finance the trade.

Indigenous traders' associations

It is possible to trade yams without being a member of the Yam Traders' Association, but it is not clear how significant this 'unregulated' trade is, and officials of the Association have an interest in emphasising its lack of importance. However, trading requires a reputation for honesty and creditworthiness, access to market information, and support in situations of crisis, which are difficult to obtain in a systematic manner outside the Association.

One useful way of understanding the membership of such an Association is that there is a core of permanent members, officials, and well-established traders who provide the continuity of the information and trading networks of the Association. Then there is a more fluid periphery of more recent members, and less successful traders, who are not able to fulfil their membership obligations, and those who are hoping to join the Association when they have accumulated the necessary resources. This fluidity at the margins of the Association is also related to the unpredictability of trade and the retreat of particular traders from this demanding trade, as their resources fall and they are replaced by others with greater resources (Clark, 1994, p.219).

An important question is who can join the Association, with its potential benefits. Only those who live in the town can become members of the Association. They also need assistance with duties such as child care. This is recognised by the provision of a day-care centre for members by the Yam Traders' Association. There is a membership fee and weekly dues of around C200, which require appropriate savings and evidence of credit worthiness to join. This is obviously only open to women with some access to financial resources. But the most important resource required to become a member of the Association is the informal one of 'reputation' and connections. There is anecdotal evidence that the Association limits membership to enhance the potential advantages of the trade for existing members but the pressure from traders wishing to join, and willingness to accept them, is greater in an expanding market such as Techiman. The present membership is 500 traders.

Control of trade

The by-laws of the market associations regulate trade by specifying that yams can only be traded in the Market, and specifying who can engage in the trade in yams. Also, no trade in yams by members is supposed to take place without the Yam Association Committee being aware of the transaction. This control makes it problematic for member traders to compete with each other in terms of price. The differentiation between traders is thus based on their long-term links with particular suppliers, and their accumulated capital and access to credit which determines the scale of their trade. It is difficult to assess how far these regulations are followed.

Evidence from the research being undertaken by the authors indicates that the expansion of the market at Techiman has created a situation, for the present, in which it is in the interest of the majority of participants, 'travellers', yam traders, and transporters, to abide by the regulations of the trading associations regarding pricing and control of trade most of the time (which is not necessarily true for less dynamic yam marketing systems in other parts of Brong Ahafo Region).

The market associations do not provide credit to their members, except in emergencies, but membership is likely to make it easier to obtain credit. One of the great expressed needs of traders is for credit, both for social purposes such as school fees and also to extend their lines of trade.

Social support networks

Members of the market association in Techiman are expected to help sick members, especially those who have children, and to provide a financial contribution for funerals. This system of social support provided to members by their association suggests that this 'cushion' for unpredictability, and the network of support in key life events, is perceived as an important factor in enabling traders to respond to rapidly changing market conditions. It also suggests that the women, such as traders, who have the resources to enter the yam trade, are in addition using those resources to establish themselves as part of an increasingly comprehensive social support network (Clark, 1994, p.228, Dennis,1991). This support network cannot be fully entered by members without the resources to make funeral contributions.

There is an economic rationale for this provision; it improves a trader's credit rating to be a visible part of an economic and social network which indicates credit-worthiness and honesty. It also demonstrates a recognition of the uncertainty, unpredictability, and impermanence of trading networks and traders' lives. These are also characteristics of other women's lives, especially in a period of prolonged restructuring of the economy.

Externally-funded alternative organisations

The women who are not able to trade and join trading associations because they lack the necessary experience, financial resources, and connections, or live in communities without specialised market systems, are those who are targeted by the credit, processing, and other income-generating groups which have been established by a wide range of organisations in Ghana: PAMSCAD, IFAD through FNOWID (Enhancing Opportunities for Women in Development), Government of Ghana through 31st December Women's Movement, foreign and indigenous NGOs, and religious institutions. The activities and organisation of these groups are strikingly similar in view of the variety of funding sources, and can be classified as 'credit' or 'processing' groups, with the credit usually being provided for trading. The credit groups are nearer in organisation and activities to the traders' associations and indigenous *susu* rotating credit groups.

There are indications from our research that the credit groups are likely to have a commitment to assist members with personal crises and funerals, whereas the processing groups do not. Women who do not possess the range of resources necessary to enter a trading association are now being given the opportunity to earn an income through externally-funded processing groups, which do not address the social needs regarded as crucial by trading associations. If this reflects the more general situation, it means that in externally sponsored women's groups in Ghana, a distinction is emerging between those which model themselves on the indigenous trading and credit groups, and those which do not.

Traders' demand for credit has an impact on externally sponsored women's organisations. There is some evidence that, in the Ghanaian situation, organisations concerned with the distribution of rural credit for women understandably tend to favour established traders' associations because of the greater possibility of the credit being repaid, thus improving repayment rates. The market associations of Techiman are associated with the Credit Union which for historical reasons is especially active in Techiman. Credit associations, such as those established by PAMSCAD and IFAD, also tend to provide loans for traders and food processors.

The initial period of membership of these associations is used to establish the potential borrowers' credibility. In spite of their unpredictability, trade and processing raw materials for trade have a quicker and more certain repayment period than agriculture, which works to a longer, more unpredictable cycle. In addition, women farmers often lack the security which would enable them to obtain credit. In the research we are undertaking in Atebubu, it has been impossible to find externally sponsored credit groups lending to women farmers, in spite of this being an area in which women play an important role in agriculture and lending to them is one of the stated objectives of donors.

There are signs that in an economy in which women's trading associations are well established and there are traditions of borrowing for trade, external funders wishing to introduce credit groups tend to use trading associations as models, by only lending to traders and processors, but ignore their social support provisions.

Conclusion

This experience suggests that trading associations, with their regulation of trading relationships and social provision for members, can under specific conditions, preside over considerable expansion and innovation in the trading system with possible benefits for farmers and urban consumers. Some of the 'specific conditions' are the result of government policy on infrastructural investment and price deregulation.

The case of Techiman also suggests that it will be difficult for externally funded women's groups to replicate the flexibility and the range and depth of support provided for their members by these associations. The combination of permanence and fluidity of membership in the Yam Traders' Association contrasts with the situation in externally established credit groups, which police their members and control their access to other organisations much more rigidly. However, requirements of membership of the Yam Traders' Association would preclude members being drawn from the very poorest sections of the community.

What is the relationship between the market traders' largely successful attempt to limit price competition between members and control trade, and the rapid expansion of the market? It is possible that the market has expanded despite the attempt to 'manage' the trade in yams, which implies that the control exercised by the Yam Traders' Association is ineffective. This does not correspond to observation. Alternatively, it can be argued that, given the favourable circumstances of improving transport, increased demand in Accra, and improved climatic conditions, the 'management' of the market by the traders' association has been one of the important factors in enabling the rapid expansion to take place.

It may be that some regulation of social and economic relationships is necessary to provide the confidence for traders to expand their operations and risk in a trading system. This would be supported by evidence from other West African market systems. It raises questions about the universal applicability of the neo-classical, free-market approaches which have dominated development debate and policy in recent years. In this perspective, government is allocated a minimal regulatory role, and organisations which try to control entry to trade and limit price competition have no place.

The second characteristic of the market association by-laws also indicates that a dynamic and expanding marketing system has more complex characteristics and variety than is indicated in a simple free-market model of economic activity, which does not recognise the importance of social support networks.

A significant difference between indigenous women's organisations and those sponsored by donors and government to carry out their policies, may be that the former are likely to be multi-purpose and the latter more limited in scope, which may have implications for the women who join them. The setting-up of processing groups which do not have a commitment to socially supporting their members in times of crisis raises questions about the possible contribution of such initiatives to sustainable income-generation, and what supplementary support networks may be necessary for poor women in more isolated communities if they are to achieve a sustainable livelihood.

External funders may have learned the 'wrong' lesson from indigenous trading associations. They have not replicated their wide social provision for members, but they have learned that it is less risky, and repayment rates are better, if credit is provided for trade rather than agricultural production, in spite of their stated objectives. The development of appropriate strategies for providing support to non-traders and processors may be arrested by this focus.

Carolyne Dennis works at the Development and Project Planning Centre, University of Bradford. Ernestina Peprah works at the Bureau of Integrated Rural Development, University of Science and Technology, Kumasi, Ghana

References

Clark G and Manuh T (1991) 'Women Traders in Ghana and the Structural Adjustment Programme', in Gladwin C (ed.) *Structural Adjustment and African Women Farmers*, Gainsville, University of Florida.

Clark G (1994) *Onions Are My Husband: Survival and Accumulation by West African Marketwomen*, Chicago, University of Chicago Press.

Dennis C (1991) 'The concept of a 'career' in Nigeria: individual perceptions of the relationship between the formal and the informal sectors', in Elson D, *Male Bias in Development Planning*, Manchester, Manchester University Press.

Moser C (1993) *Gender Planning and Development: Theory, Practice and training*, London, Routledge and Kegan Paul.

Robertson C (1983) 'The death of Makola and other tragedies: male strategies against a female-dominated system', *Canadian Journal of African Studies*, 17(3): 469-95.

Sarris A and Shams H (1991) *Ghana Under Structural Adjustment in Agriculture: The Impact on Agriculture and the Rural Poor*, New York, New York University Press.

SPRING Programme (1989) *Techiman District Study: A Development Plan for Techiman Department of Planning*, Kumasi, University of Science and Technology.

Gendered transitions: a review essay

Maxine Molyneux

Superwomen and the Double Burden: Women's Experience of Change in Central and Eastern Europe and the Former Soviet Union Chris Corrin (ed.), Second Story Press, (Canada) 1992

The Color of Gender: Re-imaging Democracy Zillah R. Eisenstein, University of California Press, (London, Berkeley) 1994

Gender Politics and Post-Communism: Reflections from Eastern Europe and the Former Soviet Union Nanette Funk and Magda Mueller (eds.), Routledge, (New York, London) 1993

Democratic Reform and the Position of Women in Transitional Economies Valentine Moghadam (ed.), Clarendon Press, (Oxford) 1993

Polish Women, Solidarity and Feminism Anna Reading, Macmillan, (London) 1992

Cinderella Goes to Market: Citizenship, Gender and Women's Movements in East Central Europe, Barbara Einhorn, Verso (London) 1993

Women in Russia: A New Era in Russian Feminism Anastasia Posadskaya (ed.), Verso (London) 1994

Women in the Politics of Postcommunist Eastern Europe, Marilyn Rueschemeyer (ed), M E Sharpe Inc, (New York and London) 1994

It is over five years since the collapse of communism in East and Central Europe; long enough for the optimism and excitement of the 'democratic revolutions' to have been dissipated by other, far less optimistic, scenarios. The costs of this great transition, still under way, have been high: as historical processes affect men and women differently, it is no surprise that many of these costs have been borne by women.

This is certainly the picture painted by this group of eight books, which is broadly representative of the body of literature on women in post-communist states that has emerged to date. If there is a common perspective uniting these otherwise varied endeavours, it is a concern to show how, in the different areas of social life, gender inequalities are being reproduced. This is not to say that things were fine under communism. On the contrary, gender asymmetries were marked then too, with women positioned as second-class citizens in a socialist political system that was itself deformed, bearing the double burden of low-paid full-time employment and arduous domestic responsibilities. So, now that this entire system has collapsed and a new one is in the process of emerging, what has changed for women?

Under communism there was the security afforded through a paternalistic state, and, for all its problems, full employment.

A commitment to formal equality in social life gave women a presence, albeit of limited significance, in the structures of bureaucratic power. Creches and kindergartens, 'mothers' allowances' and generous maternity leave payments, were aimed at reconciling the tensions created by official concern at the declining birthrates and an economic dependency on female labour.

As the distance of historical perspective makes clear, the distinctive achievement of state socialism was to include women in its modernising project. Its greatest disservice to one of the causes it claimed to promote – that of 'women's emancipation' – was to create a harsh, hypocritical, and in some ways a grossly inefficient way of doing so. The negative connotations of what some critics now call a 'forced emancipation' has worked to discredit the very idea of women's rights in the new democracies.

Those of us who first attempted to grapple with the significance for gender relations of this transition, predicted deepening gender divisions in economic and social life, the marginalisation of women from the formal institutions of political power, and a deterioration of women's reproductive and legal rights. Although this analysis was at first seen as unduly pessimistic in the post-communist states themselves, the early years of restructuring unhappily bore it out. By 1992, female unemployment was significantly higher than male in all but a few countries, and analysts were predicting a further rise, in the absence of adequate policies to deal with it. The process of the 'feminisation of poverty' was also proceeding apace, and, as in cases of economic restructuring elsewhere, women's burdens rose to compensate for the roll-back in state provisioning: creches were decimated, and the costs of health care rose.

With free elections and the end of the former quota system which guaranteed that a proportion of government positions went to women candidates, women's presence in formal politics dwindled; meanwhile, opposition to the erosion of women's rights by forces, both religious and nationalist, was either minimal or sporadic.

However, as the transition has proceeded, generalisations have begun to require qualification in the light of the emerging differences between countries, with respect to their chances for economic recovery, their particular policy environments, and the size of their 'gender gaps'.[1]

Barbara Einhorn's aptly titled *Cinderella Goes to Market* provides a comparative overview of the aftershock of the collapse of communism, with chapters on state socialism's legacy, ideologies of family and nation, reproductive rights, politics, employment, and women's movements. Her own long involvement with the German Democratic Republic (GDR) as scholar, feminist, and peace activist enables her to draw out both the similarities and the differences between countries within her thematic schema. While Hungary, Poland, Czechoslovakia, and Germany before and after unification, provide the empirical core of the volume, references are made, where appropriate, to other post-communist states.

The differences of history, cultural formation, and economy have already marked out separate paths for the more prosperous states of Hungary, the Czech Republic, and now unified Germany. While women are virtually absent from institutional politics in the first two, the German Bundestag enjoys one of the highest proportions of women in Parliament anywhere in Europe (and that had already reached one-fifth by 1990). If, as Einhorn suggests, this is the product of 20 years of debate in the West about women's place in society, (notably absent in the East), the former GDR had itself achieved impressive rates of social provision by virtue of its relatively stronger economy. Meanwhile, Catholic Poland and the Slovak Republic have seen the active influence of religious forces in the struggle over restricting reproductive rights, with the Polish leadership being able to engineer the passage of the what are among the most repressive abortion laws in the Western world.

Other significant contrasts emerge in the edited collections of Funk and Mueller, Moghadam, Corrin, and Reuschemeyer, all of which provide interim analyses of a range of countries and issues, as well as some attempts at theoretical reflection. Corrin's book has chapters on Hungary, Poland, the Czech and Slovak Republics, the GDR, former Yugoslavia and the former USSR. While this collection, having been compiled in the early years of the transformation, inevitably has more on the past than the period since 1989, it serves as a useful introduction to the themes and to the region as a whole, with an effort to present the available data on a range of social issues.

The collections compiled by Moghadam, Funk and Mueller, and Reuschemeyer offer a broad-ranging assortment of topics and authors from both West and East. There is some overlap of authors as between the volumes, with familiar names appearing in each. Moghadam's consists of 14 articles arranged in three broad sections: democratisation, perestroika in the USSR, and economic reform and women's employment. Authors include regional specialists such as Wolchik, Lapidus, Heynes, and Einhorn, along with local scholars from Russia (Posadskaya, Bodrova), Poland (Ciechocinska) and Bulgaria (Kostova). Usefully, this book includes contributions from advisers who work within international agencies such as the World Bank and the ILO, and whose advocacy of the market includes recommendations to strengthen women's competitive position within it. Fong and Paull for instance, advisors to the World Bank, call for the real freeing up of women's labour by, among other things, the provision of extensive childcare arrangements. However, Paukert, from the ILO, analysing trends in women's employment, predicts a deepening divide between low-paid jobs, mostly filled by women and subject to increasing casualisation, and jobs with better pay, conditions, and prospects, which will be largely filled by men.

Funk and Mueller's is the collection with the greatest range, containing 30 articles including the editors' introduction. There are sections on every region, except Albania, and the articles are written mostly by local scholars. Authors are as diverse in perspective as they are in origin, and this book succeeds in giving a real sense of the varying concerns and priorities of those writing on women's issues. Some offer positions which Funk and Mueller concede Western feminists, including themselves, might find difficult to support; Harsanyi for instance argues against 'importing' Western feminism, seen as 'yet another foreign theory'. Yet these are old debates within feminism, and it is perhaps inevitable that they will be played out again in the relatively new terrain of Eastern Europe, as issues of principle and practice acquire their own distinctive regional cast.

Rueschemeyer's collection is concerned with the question of politics, broadly defined. With the exception of Wolchik's chapter, one by the editor herself on the former GDR, and one co-authored piece, most of the nine articles are by women who are, at least in origin, from the regions they write about. There are strong articles by Silva Meznaric and Mirjane Ule (comparing Croatia and Slovenia), by Eva Fodor (on Hungary) and full discussions of less commonly-researched countries such as Bulgaria and Albania. These studies show how the new 'male-democracies' have consistently ignored or overridden women's concerns. Women have not only been marginalised within the realm of institutionalised politics; this marginalisation is mirrored in the weak presence of women's movements which are rarely able to carry women's demands into the policy arena. Politics is a masculine domain; it has not shaken off its old negative connotations. It is not only unattractive to women but, as far as the general public is concerned, women are not seen as suited to political life. While some authors see hope in women's greater activity at local level they recognise that this is far from the centres of decision making.

Yet the theme which these books return to again and again is the overwhelming sense of insecurity felt by women in a context of job loss, declining incomes, and a deteriorating social environment in which crime is rising daily. Open discrimination against women and what Sharon Wolchik (in Rueuschemeyer) sees as a 'backlash' against 'emancipation from above', have produced a policy environment distinctly unfriendly to women, let alone to feminist concerns.

However, in spite of all this, no-one wants to put the clock back. The old system may no longer be condemned as all bad, and the honeymoon with liberalism may be over. The liberal freedoms now in place are seen as a mixed blessing in the context of inadequate social supports, and democratic deficits, but they are seen as a blessing nonetheless. There is the freedom to make money as well as the freedom to starve; there is the freedom to vote the government out, to form associations, and to 'do politics'. But this poses the question of whether this is a freedom that women will be able to take advantage of. The evidence so far is largely negative. The process of moving to a market economy, given women's peculiar 'embeddedness' in the reproductive sphere, is already having different effects on women and men; the old adage 'to those that have, more will be given' would seem to sum up the emerging pattern.

It is, therefore, overwhelmingly men who are the beneficiaries of the privatisation policies, and who are making the real money in the new market economies. Women's businesses may be on the increase, but they are small and underfunded, their owners overburdened, and deprived of training and lucrative contracts. Women's employment is concentrated in low-waged areas, and privatisation has favoured the employee who comes unencumbered with what are derisively called 'women's privileges', i.e. maternity and childcare leave. More generally, the move to a liberal market economy has entailed a redefinition of women's rights as citizens, with a corresponding reduction or loss of previous entitlements in the areas of public welfare and employment.

Anna Reading's book of interviews with Polish women fleshes out the detail of women's experiences of transition. Women workers, managers, medics, politicians, feminists, and university lecturers, candidly speak of their experiences as women living in Poland, and in so doing, underline the point that women's attitudes on issues such as reproductive rights, sexuality, pornography, and feminism are diverse. But they are more than aware of the costs that they are bearing as women of the harsh conditions imposed by restructuring. The image of womanhood represented here is not of a cowed and passive femininity, but of women making strategic choices within very difficult circumstances, well aware of the boundaries of power relations between the sexes.

Anastasia Posadskaya's collection of 12 articles by self-proclaimed feminist scholars from the Gender Institute in Moscow draws attention to the paradox of the Soviet legacy for women in Russia itself. Klimenkova, bravely bringing what she calls 'a post-modern perspective' to the analysis of women's condition, sees the totalitarian past as one which, despite the trappings of technological and scientific advance, preserved a strongly gender-differentiated culture, while forming official policies that promoted sex discrimination in the name of the socialist community.

Liberalisation and democracy did not produce a more tolerant and egalitarian set of attitudes about men's and women's roles; rather, they have deeply unsettled men and unleashed a tide of anger against women. Discourses about the need to return women to the home, to 're-feminise' women and to 're-masculinise' men, to end the 'false emancipation of women', reveal a desire to punish and to blame women. It is not clear exactly for what: 'too much emancipation' seems hardly a plausible reason. Several authors in this book see the tenfold increase in rape, the rising incidence of domestic violence against women, the denigration and fascination with women's bodies in pornography and the appalling treatment of women's issues in the media, as symptomatic of a deeply vengeful misogyny.

Yet it is here, on this unpromising Russian soil, that an independent feminist movement has grown amidst the chaos of Russian political and social life. The battles against opponents are tough enough but the movement has begun nonetheless to institutionalise itself: several successful conferences have been held, and policy statements issued and discussed. Posadskaya herself, the initiator of this process, has served as a policy adviser on a number of government committees. But the ultimate fate of the women of the Russian Federation lies in forces largely outside their control: they are closely tied to the uncertain future of Russian democracy itself. We are reminded by Eisenstein's thoughtful book that feminism's urgent task is the elaboration of democratic theory, not only to encompass the requirements of a politics which is capable of countering the structures and practices of racism and sexism, but which can thread through it feminism's concerns to promote appropriate attitudes towards reproductive rights, sexuality and the family.

The distinctiveness of these individual countries does not dispel the sense that the commonalities are still present. When it comes to gender roles this is most strikingly evident in the social conservatism of these states, which on all indicators differ from their West European counterparts. For many feminists this is the underlying puzzle of post-communist transitions – women, so long urged to think of themselves as emancipated, still do on average three times more housework than their Western counterparts, and perform more hours of paid work, while also experiencing the inequalities of low pay and discrimination at work.

This may be, as Einhorn suggests, because under communist rule, the meanings ascribed to the public/private divide are quite different in the East and the West. In the former, the private sphere, while officially ignored, was invested with the significance of a haven from, and site of resistance to, the state. While Western feminism sought both to validate women's subjective experience and to have it accepted as a matter of public concern, Eastern European women subordinated their privations in the family to an idealised notion of what the private sphere represented. The lack of debate over women's issues in the conditions of restructuring reflects the long absence, under collectivist authoritarianism, of a rights-oriented politics.

Other cultural strands play into this difference and, as Klimenkova shows, long pre-date communism. The much stronger cultural disposition to see gender attributes as natural and fundamental gives rise to a greater sympathy for a politics of difference than has been common in much of the West. The dismissal by many women in post-communist states of feminist perspectives has itself something to do with the suppression under communist rule of theoretical debate in general. The closed nature of these societies insulated them from philosophical developments taking place elsewhere. We are reminded of the stifling conformity of academic life under communism in Posadskaya's account of her struggle to be allowed to do doctoral research on feminist issues: in the event she first encountered Western feminism when her supervisor set her the task of writing a critique of it from a Soviet perspective.

It is still too early to make a definitive assessment of the effects of the combined processes of economic and political liberalisation on women, let alone on gender relations. These are countries in flux, weathering the storms of historical change, uncertain of their futures and uneasy about their pasts. Much research and theorising still needs to be done to grasp the complexity of the changes under way, and their significance to gender relations. These books testify to the richness of the field as well as to the emergence of a regional scholarship on issues of feminist concern. There are, however, some notable absences in these books when taken together. Three of these are particularly striking, and are important not only for the field of post-communist studies, but for feminist theory as a whole.

The first concerns the need to relate the analysis of post-communism to the extensive theoretical work and ongoing debate on the effects of markets on gender relations, and of economic and political liberalisation more broadly. The second is the need to effect a thorough exploration of gender relations rather than of women alone; one which necessarily includes men and masculinity and the relational aspects of gender. Men in post-communist states are also losers in the transition process. As Peggy Watson has argued,[2] there is a male identity crisis, a product of a widespread masculine anomie, reflected in the rising male suicide and mortality rates. This gender gap needs dealing with in the context of the debate about what is happening to masculinity in the modern world more generally.

Thirdly, national and internal accounts of processes affecting gender relations are insufficient. There is in this literature an absence of discussion of the international forces which are acting on the post-communist states, and which are affecting their policy environments. With IMF adjustment packages in place, membership of the European Union pending for Poland, the Czech and Slovak Republics, and Hungary – and other states applying to join – the pressures for some convergence with the more egalitarian legal framework of the EU is to be expected. Other supra-national forces, whether they be cultural, economic, social or political, occupy an important place in analyses and explanations of the construction of the new 'gender regimes' of the post-communist world. The lessons of all these books is that for women such supra-national forces have, as much as do domestic processes, profoundly contradictory effects.

Maxine Molyneux is a political sociologist who has published widely on communist and post-communist states. Her most recent articles on these themes include 'The "Woman Question" in the age of perestroika', published in R Blackburn (ed.) After the Fall, *Verso 1991; and 'Women's rights and the international context: reflections on the post-communist states' in* Millenium: A Journal of International Studies *(London) 1994.*

Notes

1 A gender gap can be defined as 'information on the different situation of the two genders, where females are systematically worse off than males' (Sara Longwe, 'Breaking the Patriarchal Bond in *Focus on Gender* 1994, 12: Oxfam).

2 Peggy Watson 'Explaining rising mortality rates among men in Eastern Europe', paper presented to the ESRC Research Seminar on Gender, Class, and Ethnicity in Eastern Europe, University of London, 1994.

INTERVIEW

Susan Cueva (centre) with members of Lingap.

Susan Cueva talks to Caroline Sweetman about migrant workers

Susan Cueva is a member of Lingap ('to care'), a grassroots organisation of Filipina migrants to the UK. Migration for work, either to a different region or to another country, is a transition faced by increasing numbers of women and men throughout the world. Currently, an estimated 1.5 million Filipina women are migrant workers overseas. Most are employed in areas traditionally associated with women – including domestic work, nursing, and 'sex work'. The dream of all migrant workers is to return home, having saved enough money for financial security. For the majority, this hoped-for transition proves unattainable.

What kind of work does Lingap do?
Currently, we are trying to set up a project to raise consciousness among women about their rights in this country. Frequently, for Filipina women, becoming more aware of their social rights, and learning to assert those rights, means having to challenge many traditional perceptions of the passive, obedient Filipina. I work in England as a community worker. It is the same kind of work that I was doing in the Philippines.

What groups were you working with in the Philippines?
Immediately before I came to England I was working in a mining area in the north of the Philippines, working with women in the community and supporting trade union activities in the mining area. Most of the people who lived in the mining camp were not originally from that place. They came from the other provinces, towns, and islands from the south of the Philippines and from the far north. Whole families accompany the men working in the mines and live in the mining camps. They send money home to relatives in the rural areas. Miners' wives tend to do bits and pieces of work, growing and selling vegetables; some work in the local export-processing factories where they receive very low wages and no unions are allowed.

Do migrants within the Philippines dream of eventual return to rural life?
Most families do not regard migrant work in the mines as permanent. They always see it as a kind of transition period for them. They work to send their children to school and college and they dream that when their children are grown up they will take them away from there, and send them back to the place where they come from. Working overseas as a migrant is seen as one way in which children can support their parents.

When I was working at the mines, back in 1985-86, a lot of the young women I was working with told me that they were going to train to be nurses. It was very expensive to study nursing in the Philippines, but the parents worked hard to pay for their nursing studies, in the hope that their children would go abroad and become nurses, and pay back the debts that their parents were burdened with. Many Filipina women, even those with professional qualifications, have to settle for work as domestic workers.

When did Filipina women begin to migrate overseas in large numbers?
In the late 1960s and early 1970s, the Philippine government had a policy of exporting workers, and Britain had a policy of importing them. There was a need for auxiliary nurses in hospitals and for workers in hotels and restaurants. Most of the workers imported by Britain from the Philippines at this time came to work in these specific sectors, and because of the kind of work, most of those who applied were women. Frequently, jobs specifically requested women applicants.

Why was that?
Traditionally, women are regarded as better at domestic work. Filipina women are stereotyped as being quiet and accepting orders. Also, women are not seen as the main breadwinner, so they will take lower wages. The migrant workers also had to state that they were single – I think because the British authorities were worried that if the workers had families, these would also want to migrate. There were about 20,000 migrants to the UK from the Philippines, and a condition attached to their work permit was that they should stay in domestic work for four years, before they could change to other jobs. Women said to themselves, 'OK, maybe during the four years I can study, and then I can change my job.' But demands for them to send money back home were very strong. A lot of women worked at two or three jobs in a day. This left little time or energy to study. And most employers did not give them the encouragement or opportunity to get further education and training.

What kind of culture shock do Filipina migrant workers experience in the UK?
People have unrealistic ideas about migrant work and what life will be like in a country such as Britain. Before I came to Britain, I thought that it was a very rich country. Workers would earn lots of money, like all the white people I had met in the Philippines. Migrant workers tend to focus on earning lots of money compared to their earnings in the Philippines. It doesn't occur to us that the cost of living is different and so is the lifestyle. I always thought I could live here like I used to live in the Philippines, where people don't need a house of their own because they can stay with friends, families, and relatives; here, you have to have your own place.

Otherwise you are forced to live on the job?
Which is what migrant domestic workers do. Many think that's OK, because it saves spending money on rent. They don't realise that they will be on call 24 hours a day.

In what ways are domestic workers exploited?
Because employers seem to think that domestic servants are people they own, command, and control, they frequently don't allow them to go out of the house; they pay them probably £40 a month, and they work them like slaves from sunrise to midnight; but they are still on call after that because sometimes they look after the children. Some of the women I have known have been physically and sexually abused by their male employers, and physically and verbally abused by their female employers.

If domestic workers can reach the police and report abuse, can they get legal help?
Migrants, especially those newly arrived, don't know anything about the law and the legal system. I know some women who were sexually abused; of course, sexual

abuse is a difficult issue to take to law, even for British women, so I have never heard of a successful case brought by a Filipina domestic worker for sexual abuse here in Britain, but I have seen a physical abuse case get compensation.

Have conditions got worse for domestic workers?
There is less regulation of working conditions. In 1980, the British Government stopped allowing migrant workers to enter the UK on work permits, so the only way they can enter is if they accompany their employers. However, the domestic workers are only given a tourist visa, so the exploitation is sanctioned in a sense, because they are not recognised as workers.

What are the barriers that prevent migrant workers returning home?
After the first four years, many migrants think 'shall I go back?' But then they ask themselves what will they do there now. The more years you are out of your country, the more you lose the chance of getting a job there. There are millions of people unemployed at home, and more and more are leaving to find work, so you think 'if I stay here at least I get some money, and I can still send money back home to my family.' That is the dilemma for women.

What about women who migrate as sexual partners?
If they cannot get a contract to go and work in Hong Kong or Singapore or Saudi Arabia as a domestic worker, then some women look to a marriage bureau. Many Filipina women say, 'if he is a nice person, then he will treat me kindly and then I could probably study and then work, and then I could help my family.' In reality a lot of cases are not like that. Although there are some genuine relationships, the men who use marriage bureaux are frequently seeking an exploitative relationship.

Is there a prejudice towards Filipina women marrying outside the community?
There is a lot of stigma for women who use marriage bureaux. This is the case even in the Filipino community which understands the poverty from which women are trying to escape. But attitudes to sexual relationships and women selling themselves are very rigid. Even in a more conventional sexual relationship, a Filipina marrying into another culture already places herself outside the community. As it is not seen as a 'real' relationship, a lot of women applying to a marriage bureau are completely isolated. Women are embarrassed to admit to their friends that they went to the marriage bureaux.

What chance does a woman have of leaving an abusive partner?
The immigration system makes it very easy for a British man to abandon the woman. She is allowed to come in for one year, and only after one year of marriage can she get a permanent visa to remain in Britain. So, at any time within that period, which sometimes lasts for 15 to 24 months, the woman has no independent status. Her husband effectively has the power to have her sent back to the Philippines.

So she cannot leave him unless she goes straight back home?
Yes, that's right. If a woman gets pregnant before obtaining a permanent visa, she still doesn't have the right to stay in the country, even if she has the child. And the man can sue for custody of the child, so the child stays and the woman is sent back home. To keep the child, you have to prove your economic means to support the child. The man can also tell the authorities that the woman is crazy. I have seen those kind of cases and really, it would drive any woman mad, having gone through those experiences and then knowing that your child will be taken away from you. These cases happen because the system allows them to happen.

What do women migrants hope for?
They tend to say they are going abroad just to earn and save enough money to be able to set up a small business in the province where they came from. They know migrant work is not forever. Even if migrant work is probably not the best solution, people dream and people hope.

Does the dream of returning home ever become a reality?
Sometimes. You don't see many return home; some of those who try end up migrants again, because they realise that there is no kind of economic hope for them at home. But, since most of us came in the 1970s and 1980s, the majority are not more than 40 or 50 years old; very few are near retirement age. I know a couple of old people who went back to the Philippines; I think they only managed it because they have adult children here, who can support them. This replicates the kind of relationship they would have if the whole family was still in the Philippines – they might have a small patch of land to plant vegetables but still they would rely on migrant labour supporting them.

Do most Filipino migrants to the UK see their children's future in Britain?
I hope myself that my children will go back to the Philippines. I always thought that the Philippines would be where my children should grow up, but now I don't know. The present economic and political situation in the Philippines is very discouraging, especially for young people. There is a dilemma; we hope that there will still be a good system of welfare in the UK, but when you see it slowly being broken down in front of your eyes, you wonder if there's any future for the children here.

What role have organisations like yours in supporting Filipina women migrants?
Filipina women would see their role as to keep the family together and pass on the traditional values of their culture. They imagine they can maintain a Filipino family just as it is in the Philippines. Our organisation tries to convey to them that in this country it is difficult to be like that. Our children brought up here are so totally different from us – we never answered our parents back or had the expectations that children have here. It is a big change for us to accept this sort of difference, so we try very hard to pull our children back towards our culture, and the children try to push us away. Our work in Lingap tries to bridge this gap between the parents and the children. There is also a role to play in offering very basic education about women's health, and women's rights in a violent relationship, because of the increasing incidence of violence in our community. We have seen some cases of Filipino children who are put into care by the government authorities, and this is a big blow – as a Filipina, I would never believe that the authorities might actually take my children away. So we have to learn about the system here, in order to come to terms with this very different situation. Lingap runs information sessions on these issues, and provides support to women, children, and other members of the family. We hope that the information and knowledge that we provide to our members can help to empower them so that they learn to take control of their situation.

Would you see the increased violence in the Filipino community as a response to crisis?
Yes. When Filipina women in Britain, who have been earning money here, bring their husbands to join them, there is a lot of pressure because the relationship has changed: the role of the breadwinner is now the woman's, while the man is dependent. When the man starts earning, there is an assumption that the woman will return to her role, doing all the housework, and, if the children need to be looked after, she will be the one to give up her job. So there is conflict in the relationship, because the women have found a sort of

independence and suddenly they lose it. They often can't express their frustration because of the years and years of socialisation. In the last ten years a lot of women who worked as senior nurses or as chambermaids have lost their jobs. In a way they become poorer than they used to be when they were here by themselves, in the sense that, not only do they not earn the money that they used to earn, but their husbands have control of the family. Lingap advises women about their right to say to their husbands or partners that they want to carry on working. In the last five years I have been working with a specific group of women, and I have seen a change in them. At first, they used to ask their husbands' permission to come to our meetings. Now they come, whether their husbands say yes or no. They come.

How do you fund your work?
At the moment, Lingap has funding from the EC, with a counterpart from Trust for London. It is hard work trying to raise money for community development activities. I worked with women in the Philippines in a project funded by Oxfam. It is much harder trying to get funding when we are working with Filipina women here in the UK. The location of work is different, of course, but that is very much part of the way global economics works. Policies of liberalisation and privatisation lose jobs both in the Philippines and the UK. Migrant labour is a result of flows in the global economic system. When we are in the UK we are just at a different point in the process.

Some international NGOs fund development education work in the UK, about the Philippines and other developing countries, though these tend to be development education projects run by education professionals, most often by white British professionals. My experience is that many international NGOs do not direct their funding at migrant organisations, who are well placed to work with the UK public on development issues. I am happy that Oxfam UK/I is developing its work in Britain now, and I hope that it will not overlook the possibility of seeking partnership with different grassroots migrant organisations like ours.

Are there any recommendations that you would make, either for people who are doing similar to your work or for those who are funding it? Are there any recommendations about best practice, what works and what doesn't?
It is very important to be sensitive to people's experiences and to people's knowledge of what's happening within the community and within themselves. What I have found very, very difficult has been when a kind of imposition is put on us living here about what is good for us and what is not good for us.

Coming from what quarters?
From different NGOs working supposedly in conjunction with developing community organisations. I have found that this kind of attitude is very prevalent: that they know best, because this is their society and they know the system. People like myself and people in my community are expected to be always at the receiving end of knowledge and resources. I think that there has to be respect for our experience and knowledge. It is not for them to say, 'this is what you should do.' It's time for development agencies to rethink their attitudes and ways of working, to become conscious of other people's experience and skills. We don't want to be patronised, we don't want to be stereotyped, we want to be respected. We have contributed quite a lot to British society. We must be respected and recognised for that contribution.

Resources

BOOK REVIEW

Arms to Fight, Arms to Protect: Women speak out about Conflict

Olivia Bennett, Jo Bexley, Kitty Warnock (eds)
Panos, London, 1995

This book is published as part of the Panos women and conflict oral testimony project and comprises the personal stories of some 85 women from 12 countries, with brief introductions to each country. It is not easy reading – sometimes because of the harrowing nature of the stories themselves, sometimes because of the dense testimony format – but is an invaluable collection and needs to be read and thought about by anyone involved in issues of conflict, whether as a policy maker, student, or relief and development practitioner. Though primarily a book about conflict, it also raises broader questions about the role of NGOs and about gender relations.

The value of the book lies in its honesty – the direct presentation of what women think – and its rendition of complexity and difference. Women are not seen as stereotypes, nor is war presented as a uniform experience, but rather as something which can have a variety of meanings. A broad difference emerges between those wars that were seen to have a purpose: the struggle of Nicaraguans, Vietnamese, and Tigrayans, for example, and which women chose, in different ways, to join; and those that were felt to be imposed from outside. The book does not glorify or exonerate, but it shows how sometimes war opened up opportunities for women and created positive changes in relations between men and women; changes that were sometimes later betrayed.

Among the strengths of the book is its sense of history. Accounts from India at the time of partition, from the Vietnam war, from Nicaragua, move us beyond the frame of reference of recent events, and help us to understand better how war happens, and perhaps what steps can be taken towards preventing it. The stories take us beyond the headlines into the long-term destruction: 'The real experience of the war is not the shelling and so on, those are just moments, though they are the ones you see on TV. War is what happens afterwards, the years of suffering hopelessly with a disabled husband and no money, or struggling to rebuild when all your property has been destroyed', says Marie from Lebanon. Nam, from Vietnam, explains the dreadful effects of Agent Orange on her family, whilst Sabaah, from Somaliland, is one of the many women who talk of how war destroys society, especially in its effects on young people. Yet she also has hope; not hope in some vague sense of wishfulness but hope that links to concrete actions and ideas of ways forward, and which has the courage to transcend the awfulness.

Women reach out from these pages in many ways. Some are there as victims of rape – most harrowingly in Bosnia, in stories that chill even after long exposure to newspaper coverage. What makes these accounts valuable is the way they connect to other women's stories and so force us to consider the wider issue of male violence against women. Women are also there as mothers and wives: searching for missing husbands; coping with pain; looking after children, or giving them up in order to join the struggle. They are there as fighters and as peacemakers – and sometimes they are there saying that peace cannot come, that they cannot forgive. 'I hope there will never be peace', says Umm Hamad, a refugee in Lebanon, 'I hope for total destruction for them and for us'. To read her story is to understand that there can be no peace unless the injustice that causes war is rooted out. Women are there, too, as refugees, and one of my strongest memories of the book is the pain of being a refugee – a pain which cuts through previous distinctions of wealth or education.

Finally, women talk of their responsibility: 'People feel that it was "other people's war", and they say the government is responsible for peace. But it is us, the citizens. We were responsible for war, we are responsible for peace', says Laure from Lebanon, and a number of women speak of some of the steps that must be taken to make that a reality. They deserve to be listened to.

Review by Chris Johnson, Communications Officer on Oxfam UK/I's Middle East Desk.

Relevant organisations

Women in Development Initiatives (IWID)
IWID seeks to strengthen the efforts of NGOs in India to empower women, through training and workshops to enhance awareness, knowledge, and skills on women's development and human rights; participatory action research on the programmes and structures of organisations; facilitation of research on critical issues for women's development; documentation and dissemination of information on gender and development; and strengthening of national and regional forums of women in NGOs to improve women's status in wider society.
Ranjani Krishnamurthy, E2, B Block, 4th floor, Parsn Paradise Apartments, 109 G.N. Chetty Road, T Nagar, Madras 600 017, India.

Asia Women's Human Rights Council Regional Secretariat
AWHRC is a region-wide network of women's organisations and human rights centres and programmes, set up in 1986 to create an Asian Women's Commission of Human Rights. Prioritised issues are: state violence and militarism, feminisation of poverty, health and survival, occupational hazards of women workers, prostitution and sex tourism, domestic violence and rape, peace and nuclear issues, environment, law, religion and culture, and the effects of fundamentalism and communalism on women.
PO Box 190, 1099 Manila, Philippines; tel/fax: (632) 921 5571 and (632) 999 437

Jerusalem Center for Women (JCW)
JCW, formed in March 1994, is a Palestinian NGO which aims to coordinate a network of Palestinian, Israeli, Arab and international women's organisations for the advancement of the peace process. JCW works parallel to its sister organisation, Bat Shalom, the centre for Israeli women. The two centres carry out joint ventures, such as community work groups for young women and a Palestinian-Israeli Dialogue Group, through their coordinating body, the Jerusalem Link.
Beit Hanina, Dahiet Al-BaridAl-Hirbawi Building, Fourth Floor, Jerusalem, PO Box 51630; tel: 02-9980068; fax: 02-9980069

Women's Information and Documentation Centre

Information exchange and networking via email in Eastern Europe is a key development in strengthening links between women's organisations in a situation of rapid social and economic change.

Zenska Infoteca, Berislaviceva 14, 41000 Zagreb, Croatia; fax: +385 41422926
e-mail: Zenskaino-zg@zamirzg.comlink.de

Women in Development Europe (WIDE)

WIDE carries forward research in a number of areas, including alternative economics. It also plays a co-ordinating role in linking with women's organisations in Western and Eastern Europe.

10, Square Ambriorix, B-1040 Brussels, Belgium; tel: + 32 2 732 44 10; fax: + 32 2 732 19 34 e-mail: WIDE@gn.apc.org

International Restructuring Education Network Europe (IRENE)

IRENE is an international network of NGOs and trade unions. IRENE aims to stimulate information exchange between organisations, promote the expansion of work on development education and industrial restructuring, publish research material and exert influence regarding relevant policies on the EU and its member states. The main link between members of the network is the newsletter which is published three times a year.

Stationsstraat 39, 5038 EC Tilburg, The Netherlands; tel: +31.13.351 523; fax: +31.13.350 253; e-mail: GEO2:IRENE-NETWORK

CAFRA: Caribbean Association for Feminist Research and Action

CAFRA is an autonomous umbrella association that was formed in 1985 by women's organisations across the region to cooperate and network. It spans the Dutch, English, French and Spanish-speaking Caribbean. Members are committed to understanding the relationship between the oppression of women and other forms of exploitation in society, and to working actively for change. It produces a quarterly newsletter in English and Spanish.

PO Box 442, Tunapuna Post Office, Tunapuna, Trinidad and Tobago; tel:(809) 663 8670/662 1231; fax:(809) 663 6482

Foundation for Women's Health and Development (FORWARD)

FORWARD campaigns and educates around women's health issues; in particular, female genital mutilation.

38 King St, Covent Garden, London WC2E 8JT, UK; tel: 071-379-6889

Inter-African Committee on traditional practices affecting the health of women and children

IAC is a non-governmental organisation working to promote the health of women and children in African by fighting harmful, and promoting beneficial, traditional practices, as well as playing an advocacy role. Its headquarters is in Ethiopia, and it has 24 national committees in 24 African countries.

Liaison office: 147 rue de Lausanne, CH 1202 Geneva, Switzerland; tel: 25 11/51 72 00; fax: 25 11/51 46 82

International Association for Feminist Economics

IAFE is a non-profit organisation advancing feminist enquiry of economic issues and educating economists and others on feminist points of view in the economy. *Feminist Economics*, published by Routledge, ISSN 1354-5701, is its newly-launched official journal, providing the first international forum for feminist economic debate. Publishing high-quality, peer-reviewed contributions from a wide range of intellectual traditions, it also publishes essays from cross-disciplinary and cross-country perspectives.

Department of Economics, University of Massachusetts, Amherst MA 01003, USA; tel: + 413 545 6362; fax: + 413 545 2921;
e-mail: folbre@econs.umass.edu

Responding to Conflict
The Responding to Conflict Programme offers 11-week intensive, experience-based courses for people working in areas of instability and conflict. Especially suitable for NGO staff aid workers, those concerned with rights, relief, reconstruction anddevelopment. Includes conflict analysis, group dynamics, negotiation, mediation. Some scholarships available.
Rsponding to Conflict, Selly Oak Colleges, Woodbrooke, 1046 Bristol Road, Birmingham B29 6LJ; tel: 44 0 121 415 5641; fax: 44 0 121 415 4119

Further Reading

Aslanbeigui N, Pressman S and Summerfield G (eds) *Women in the Age of Economic Transformation: Gender Impact of Reforms in Post-Socialist and Developing Countries* Routledge UK 1994
Demonstrates the gender bias of structural change and the resultant erosion of women's social and political status. Shows how women are bearing a large share of the burden of economic transformation.

Barrows L.C. (ed) *Gains and Losses: Women and Transition in Eastern and Central Europe* European Network For Women's Studies (ENWS) 1994
Provide suggestions for action on gender relations and the advancement of women at national, regional and grass-roots levels by identifying succesful pathways through political and socio-economic changes.

De Bruijn M (ed) *Advancing Women's Status: Women and Men Together?* Royal Tropical Institute Press Amsterdam 1995
An invaluable resource for gender and development practitioners. Four themes critically reviewed from a gender perspective: women's status and rights, education and training, economic participation and sexual and reproductive health. Reflects recent approaches to gender and argues for greater participation from men, seperately and together with women.

Carlson B, Langevin-Falcon C and Bondad M. *Women and Gender in Countries in Transition: A UNICEF Perspective* UNICEF 1994
Assesses the changing situation for women in Central and Eastern Europe via UNICEF's "life cycle" analysis of gender. Concludes that in most countries undergoing transition there has been a negative impact on the status of women.

Einhorn B *The Impact of the Transition from Centrally Planned Economies on Women's Employment in East Central Europe* Institute of Development Studies (IDS) UK 1993
Surveys the implications of economic transition on women's employment opportunities in the light of pre-1989 policy regarding women's economic role and the gender-biased effects of current adjustments to the market.

Ginwala F, Mackintosh M and Massey D *Gender and Economic Policy in a Democratic South Africa.* DPP Working Paper 21, Faculty of Technology. Open University, UK, 1991
Addresses the question of gender oppression in the course of the fundamental changes to society proposed by the ANC. .

Joekes S and Weston A *Women and the New Trade Agenda* UNIFEM 1994
Outlines the gender-specific results of recent trends in world trade at national, regional and international levels. Considers how women can participate in the formation of trade policy.

Moghadam V. M. *Modernising Women: Gender and Social Change in the Middle East* Lynne Rienner Publishers, Inc. 1993
Includes an analysis of the historical context to the present political transitions with specific reference to "the woman question".

Momsen J. H.(ed) *Women and Change in the Caribbean: A Pan-Caribbean Perspective* James Currey Ltd London UK 1993
A feminist interpretation of a multi-cultural society engaged in rapid change and restructuring. Focuses on women's status and gender relations in the public and private spheres and women's economic activity, with case-studies from 15 countries.

Riley M *Transforming Feminism* OP #4095 Centre for Concern, Alternative to Women in Development project Washington, D.C.
ALT-WID is a coalition of women researchers and policy advocates based in Washington, DC, working within national and international networks with the aim of bringing gender, race and class critiques to current development practice. ALT-WID are seeking alternative development processes based on the experience and empowerment of women.

Rowbotham S and Mitter S *Dignity and Daily Bread: New Forms of Economic Organising among Poor Women in the Third World And The First.* Routledge, 1993
Charts historical and contemporary collective responses of women workers to transitions in the global economy.

Rowbotham S *Women and the Global Economy* War On Want, undated
Examines the impact of global economic transition upon women, the growth of transnational corporations, and cuts in the provision of social welfare. Includes listings of women's organisations campaigning on behalf of homeworkers.

Sen G and Grown C (DAWN) *Development, Crises and Alternative Visions.* Monthly Review Press and Zed Books Ltd. 1987
A key book for development practitioners, recommending alternative development policies which reflect a feminist version of a better world.

Singh N *The Bankura Story: Rural Women Organise for Change* International Labour Organisation, New Delhi,1988, Reprinted 1993 How a women's samity (society) helped village women in West Bengal to create employment for themselves from a land donation.

Urdang S *And Still They Dance: Women, War and the Struggle for Change in Mozambique* Earthscan Publications Ltd London UK, 1989
Mozambique's independence in 1975 seemed a unique opportunity for women's liberation. Reflects the impact of destabilisation on the 'gender struggle' amid the re-building of Mozambique.

Audio/Visual Resources:

Amazon Sisters VHS 50mins 1992 G86
Testimonies of women who actively struggle in defence of their families, communities and against destructive industrial and environmental change.

Portraits of Change VHS 50mins 1991 G87
Stories of two Fillipina women who are negotiating changes in their societies and struggling against injustice and oppression.

Angola is our Country VHS 45mins undated G113
The contribution of women to the reconstruction of Angola after the wars against Portugese colonialism and the South African army.

To be a Woman VHS 42mins 1992 G112
Africa's response to economic transition, highlights the impact of structural adjustment programmes on women and children in Ghana, Uganda and Zambia.

All these videos are available for loan from the Information Centre, Oxfam, 274 Banbury Road, Oxford OX2 7DZ. Tel: 01865-312449. Please quote the reference number when ordering.